Praise for *Motivate Your Child*

"As president of an organization that works with college students, I can clearly see that we need more books like Scott and Joanne's— books that coach parents to develop strong character in their children that will last the rest of their lives."

— Alec Hill, president of InterVarsity Christian Fellowship/USA

"As a Christian psychiatrist, who takes a Bio-Psycho-Spiritual approach to diagnosis and treatment, Scott and Joanne have come through again like the cavalry to the rescue. Using sound science as a tool to break down powerful but too big biblical life management and transforma- tion principles into digestible, practical, and easy to implement action steps, they equip parents to have a divinely powerful strategy and weapon in the spiritual war for our children's minds and souls."

— Karl Benzio, MD; psychiatrist; founder and director of Lighthouse Network

"[This is] an exceptional book—a proven GPS programmed for your child's heart. The practical, real-life examples will guide you through- out the parenting journey. Your children will enjoy lifelong direction and motivation."

— Mark Steiner, president of DiscipleLand.com

"Some parenting books make me feel more guilty than empow- ered. Turansky and Miller offer practical insight to help parents find attainable ways to motivate their kids with the big picture in mind and not just the crisis at hand. Great blend of challenging us but making spiritual parenting doable."

— Ron Hunter Jr., executive director and CEO of Randall House, D6 Conference Director, and coauthor of *Toy Box Leadership*

"*Motivate Your Child* combines a solid foundation of prayer and scripture with Scott and Joanne's real-life experiences counseling hundreds of families. Begin by picturing a preferred future for your children. Learn how to tweak daily interactions to build healthy daily relationships. Free up energy the family once spent on disobedience, correction, and selfishness so together you can serve others and live in obedience to God. I strongly recommend this book!"

— Kirk Weaver, president of Family Time Training

"*Motivate Your Child* is a book that I recommend to you because of how it helped me as a father. God used the scriptures that Turansky and Miller share to give me a greater passion—and a sharper plan—to help my children develop a godly, Scripture-driven conscience, which will serve them throughout their lives."

— Dr. Rob Rienow, Visionary Family Ministries

"[This is] a compelling book that can easily become the go-to resource for parents hoping to intentionally raise up children who make good choices for the right reasons and who become adults who live out their faith in Jesus Christ with integrity and compassion."

— Rev. Dr. Orlando Crespo, national director of InterVarsity Latino Fellowship (LaFe)

motivate your child

motivate your child

A Christian Parent's Guide to
Raising Kids Who Do What They
Need to Do Without Being Told

Dr. Scott Turansky and
Joanne Miller, RN, BSN

NELSON
BOOKS

An Imprint of Thomas Nelson

Published in Nashville, Tennessee, by Nelson Books, an imprint of Thomas Nelson. Nelson Books and Thomas Nelson are registered trademarks of HarperCollins Christian Publishing, Inc.

Thomas Nelson titles may be purchased in bulk for educational, business, fund-raising, or sales promotional use. For information, please e-mail SpecialMarkets@ThomasNelson.com.

Unless otherwise noted, Scripture is taken from the Holy Bible, New International Version®, NIV®. Copyright © 1973, 1978, 1984, 2011 by Biblica, Inc.™ Used by permission of Zondervan. All rights reserved worldwide. www.zondervan.com

Scripture quotations marked ESV are taken from THE ENGLISH STANDARD VERSION. © 2001 by Crossway Bibles, a division of Good News Publishers.

Scripture quotations marked KJV are taken from the Holy Bible, King James Version (public domain).

All emphasis in Scripture quotations are the authors' own.

The names of people who have come to the National Center for Biblical Parenting for counseling have been changed. Some illustrations combine individual stories in order to protect confidentiality. Stories of the authors' children have been used by permission.

Library of Congress Cataloging-in-Publication Data

Turansky, Scott, 1957–
  Motivate your child : a Christian parent's guide to raising kids who do what they need to do without being told / by Dr. Scott Turansky and Joanne Miller, RN, BSN.
    pages cm
  Includes bibliographical references and index.
  ISBN 978-0-529-10073-3
1. Child rearing—Religious aspects—Christianity. 2. Parenting—Religious aspects—Christianity. 3. Obedience—Religious aspects—Christianity. I. Title.
  BV4529.T885 2015
  248.8'45—dc23   2014023482

Printed in the United States of America

15 16 17 18 19 RRD 6 5 4 3 2 1

Contents

Part 2: Spiritual Development in Children

Introduction

Imagining the Destination

Happiness may be found in the destination,
but character is built in the journey.

The camera pans across snow-capped mountains, zoom-ing in on a resort with happy skiers on the Colorado ski slopes. The scene then shifts to a sandy beach in Hawaii, with two people laughing as they play in the waves. As you watch the beauty, you wonder, *What is this commercial about, anyway? It sure looks inviting.* At that same moment your answer comes on the screen. It's an advertisement for a travel agency.

When a travel company creates a commercial, they don't display the inside of their office. Instead, they show you where they can take you and the places you can go. Delightful beaches, majestic mountains, and exotic locations provide a vision of new possibilities.

In the same way, we want to invite you to take the next few minutes to catch a vision for what happens to you and your family when you work on internal motivation with your kids. Frankly, you'll likely need to make some changes in the way you parent, so it's helpful to get the bigger picture. When you recognize the impact by looking at the destination, you're more likely to make the commitment.

In this book you'll learn how to develop self-motivation in your children. When parents deliberately work on spiritual and moral development, their kids accumulate new resources in their hearts. The heart contains a child's operating principles.

God's GPS

Moral and spiritual development increase internal motivation. Amazing things happen when you teach and train your child in those two areas. Specific parenting strategies will adjust common relating patterns, and you'll watch the changes take place in your child's heart.

If you imagine the destination, you'll think about where you want your child to be in twenty-five years. Close your eyes and try to think into the future. What will your child be like? Do you think of a job or marriage? Who knows what that might be like? But you can also imagine things like integrity, a strong work ethic, responsibility, and a healthy faith. If your son or daughter has those things, then whatever else comes, your child will be prepared. Keeping the destination in mind provides you with greater motivation in the challenges you face and the decisions you'll make in the next year, month, week, and even today.

We know you want your kids to be successful. That's why you carefully consider schooling options, encourage extracurricular activities, and help your children choose friends wisely. But some parents define "successful" as having a good job and being happy in life. They confuse the destination with the journey. If you try to give your kids the destination by providing them with all the toys that come with human success, you may find that your kids lack the character to manage them.

On the other hand, parents who emphasize the journey are able to help their kids understand life, work through the challenges, and know how to read the map. In time, those kids not only arrive at the destination of godly success but they understand how they got there and what's important in life.

Parenting is the process of giving children the tools to navigate

> A problem takes place when parents confuse the destination with the journey.

life. Speaking of tools, a GPS is a wonderful invention. It can help guide a driver from one place to another, avoid the traffic, and find various attractions along the way. But a GPS is only as valuable as the data it relies upon. It's not uncommon to follow the GPS to the promised Mexican restaurant, only to find a vacant lot or a residential area.

One couple, driving their SUV from Klamath Falls, Oregon, got stuck in a huge snowstorm for three days because they followed their GPS. The little device told them to take a small road as a shortcut through the mountains to get where they wanted to go. Unfortunately, the dirt road wasn't such a good idea after all. It wound endlessly through the mountains and when the snowstorm hit, became impassable. The GPS had indicated the shortest route, but in this case, it wasn't the safest route. The lure of a shortcut led this couple into an unwanted detour.

We know you'd like your child to be more self-motivated when you're trying to get out the door in the morning, or when your child is working on homework, doing chores, or trying to develop kindness toward his or her siblings. You'll learn how to build that internal motivation in the coming chapters. But it's important to understand where the internal sense of responsibility and compassion comes from. Some good theology about the human heart can produce great application for daily chores and activities. You'll apply this theology to your kids whether they are preschoolers, elementary age, or teens. As you read further, we'll move back and forth between a long-term vision for your kids and dealing with the everyday responsibilities of life.

> Some good theology about the human heart can produce great application for daily chores and activities.

God has created an internal GPS inside the human heart. It's made up of two things: a strong faith and a good conscience. The two work together to help you accurately navigate the roads of life, so you'll choose not simply the most convenient path, but the wisest one. They help you make choices based on internal conviction instead of simply acting to get some kind of reward. Don't just take our word for it. Let's look at the Scriptures.

Paul, in encouraging young Timothy to be wise in navigating his own life, described faithfulness this way: "holding on to faith and a good conscience." He went on to say, "Some have rejected these and so have shipwrecked their faith" (1 Timothy 1:19). Of all the things Paul could have used to describe the difference between those who stay the course and those who shipwreck their faith, he picked these two: *faith* and *a good conscience*. These two internal navigation tools were designed to maneuver the human heart through the challenges of life.

The purpose of this book is to define those two tools and to provide you with hands-on strategies to give each of your children an accurate and reliable GPS for his or her heart. Passing on the faith to kids and helping them each develop a clear and strong conscience are strategic for success in life. The Holy Spirit uses these tools as he directs a person and guides that individual's everyday actions.

It's not very helpful to look at a map after you've already reached the end of your journey. It's more beneficial to use it as a tool to get from where you are to where you need to be. Children can understand map reading and navigation as parents walk through life with them. There's a lot to learn about plotting the best route and then changing course to avoid problems, or hanging in there to overcome them. Some of the dangerous curves or hidden icebergs are hard to see in advance without a navigational tool. Ships run aground and cars go over cliffs because of poor navigation.

When parents provide the destination without the navigation, kids often don't develop character and thus lack the tools necessary for success. On the contrary, when parents teach their children how to navigate life and anchor their decisions based on God's signposts and directions, their kids can find their way to new heights and uncharted territory. In this book, we'll show you how.

It's All About the Heart

The heart, as the Bible defines it, is a complex piece of equipment placed inside of every person. Jesus said in Matthew 12:34, "Out of the overflow of the heart the mouth speaks." The reality is that problems happen in the heart before they happen in behavior. That was much of Jesus' message in the Sermon on the Mount. For example, he warned of the similarity between anger, which begins in the heart, and murder. They're both forms of revenge. Of adultery he said, "Anyone who looks at a woman lustfully has already committed adultery with her *in his heart*" (Matthew 5:28, emphasis added).

A huge piece of internal motivation is beliefs, and those beliefs reside inside the heart and impact daily decision making. Every week as you interact with your children regarding spiritual things, you'll contribute to their healthy spiritual understanding of God, the world, and their own hearts. And because you're doing it over time, your children's spiritual lives will become integrated into what they do and how they think.

Furthermore, children are developing their moral character at a rapid rate. They're determining in their hearts the difference between right and wrong. The fibers of morality grow together to make each of your children into the person that God intended. It doesn't happen by accident. Moral and spiritual development happen together, and the work you do makes a lasting impact. Conscience development, however, is more than just moral development. It helps children develop a sense of responsibility. Consider the following examples.

Ricardo is five years old. He has a hard time following instructions and often has a bad attitude. Dad must discipline him regularly for his poor responses.

At one point, Dad sat down with Ricardo and explained why having a bad attitude is a problem. "Ricardo," he said, "you're going to be receiving instructions for the rest of your life. Sometimes you won't want to do what's asked. One of the jobs God designed for you in our family is to learn how to follow instructions with a good attitude. Hidden within obedience are the secret ingredients you'll need to be successful in life. So we're going to practice following instructions with a good attitude in a way that pleases your mom and me and God."

Every night, when Dad tucked Ricardo into bed, he prayed that God would make Ricardo strong so he could follow instructions with a good attitude. He used a multifaceted approach to helping his son change, including discussion, firmness, prayer, and practice. Framing the picture, along with a lot of daily work, helped Ricardo make significant changes in his attitude toward following instructions.

A mother believed that her daughter, Su, age thirteen, was too consumed with electronics. Mom realized that the real spiritual issue had to do with Su wanting to please herself instead of thinking about others. Mom decided to limit computer and video game time and met with her daughter to plan ways to think of others, both around their home and outside the family. She said to her daughter, "God helped the Philippians learn to think of others. In a letter Paul wrote to them, he said, 'Do nothing out of selfish ambition . . . , but in humility consider others better than yourselves. Each of you should look not only to your own interests, but also to the interests of others.' We want to be like that too." Together they planned ways to value others, and each evening Mom would ask Su, "What act of kindness did you do today?" Mom used the Scriptures in a positive way to help her daughter see that her purpose in life was not to have fun but to serve others.

Juan, age nine, was mean to his six-year-old brother, Carlos. Carlos was annoying, and everyone knew it. Juan believed that if his brother was annoying, he had the right to be mean to him. After all, he deserved it. Dad and Mom decided to make some changes. They wanted to help Juan develop the kind of compassion Jesus had. Instead of setting up threats and punishment plans, they decided that every evening before bed, they would go into his room, and together with Juan, they would pray for Carlos. Juan and his parents prayed that Carlos would learn to be more aware of how his actions were irritating to others.

After a few days of praying, they began seeing changes in Juan. The way he related to his brother changed. He was more willing to help Carlos see what was annoying and to suggest to him what he could do differently. When asked about it, Juan said, "I used to get angry with Carlos, and then I would get mean. But now I'm not angry. I feel sorry for him, and so I just ask him to cut it out, and he does."

Ricardo, Su, and Juan all made changes in their lives because their parents used a heart-based approach. Most children will need several strategies, such as firmness, correction, consequences, and teaching, but in the midst of all that, there must be a core that helps them change their hearts, not just their behavior. Parents must see to it that their children are internally motivated, instead of relying on externals, such as reward and punishment, to motivate them.

> Level two thinking advances responsibility in kids at any age.

As you read on you'll learn about three levels of thinking that contribute to moral and spiritual development. Level one thinking is what kids engage in every day, thinking about themselves and their own activities. Level two thinking advances responsibility in kids at any age. It focuses on other people, other tasks, and time. Level three thinking considers what God might be doing in the present situation, further increasing a child's maturity. These higher levels of thinking increase internal motivation. When you adjust your parenting strategies to enhance these other levels of thinking, you will maximize the work you do in your child's heart.

This book keeps an eye on the destination, but it's really about tools for the journey. We'll help you determine what's required to get there and then break the solutions down into steps that you can take with your kids. As you read this book, you'll discover new ideas and strategies. You may find affirmation for some of the things you're already doing well. You may also be challenged to adjust some of the ways you're currently working with your kids. We know that amazing things will happen. Strategic conversations with your kids will mark pivotal points of change, but they will come because of the daily work you do to continually point your child in the right direction, provide opportunities to think in godly terms, and discipline in ways that teach, not just punish.

As we study internal motivation with you in this book, we'll give you practical ways to put it all into practice. We'll discuss how to use consequences in a heart-based approach, ways to maximize the words you say to your child so that they impact the heart, and how to energize your devotions so your kids will learn to hear from God.

In short, you're leading your kids on an adventure through life. Every day they learn from you, watch how you work, and respond to your expectations. In the first chapters of this book you'll learn some valuable theology about the human heart that will launch you into exciting solutions for building self-motivation in your children.

PART 1

Moral Development in Children

1

Internal Versus External Motivation

*External motivation has this way of squelching
initiative, decreasing creativity, and robbing
one of the satisfaction of accomplishment.*

Anna and Dave Correra were frustrated every morning trying to get their three kids out the door. It was as if each one of the children needed a personal assistant to keep moving. These parents often joked that their kids needed assisted living as much as Grandma did in the rest home.

Dad and Mom wished their children would be internally motivated to do what's right instead of relying on parental prompters to get things done. Instead, their kids waited for instructions for each task. "Are you dressed?" "Did you eat breakfast?" "Brush your hair." "Get your backpack by the door." "Where are your shoes?" And on and on it went. Dad and Mom realized that they were functioning as the conscience for each of their kids, prompting them forward each step of the way. It was time for a change.

Dave and Anna didn't like the nagging and were frustrated by the patterns that had developed. Their kids needed to learn a better way. In a moment we'll tell you what they did, but first some background to understand their new methodology.

Developing the Conscience

The study of moral development in children doesn't come from a psychology textbook. It comes from the Bible. In order to maximize parenting, it's important to view children from a biblical perspective and understand how they're designed. The purpose of the conscience is to reveal to every person that God exists and that there is a right and a wrong.

In subsequent chapters we'll share with you practical ways to use the conscience in your parent training to build internal motivation. In chapter 4, we'll show you how you can use conscience training to increase responsibility in a child of any age. In chapter 5, you'll learn how to help kids take responsibility for offenses instead of blaming them on others. In chapter 7, you'll learn how to use the conscience to help kids overcome selfish tendencies and consider others. A study of the conscience arms parents with a whole new toolbox for parent training. But before we get to some of the tools, let's continue with some more theology so you can embed your parental activity into your faith.

It's fair to say that God placed the conscience inside a person to provide an internal motivation to find God and give one's heart to him. The conscience is on a mission, and only when it finds salvation through Jesus Christ is it satisfied. After salvation, though, what use is the conscience? Is that the end of its purpose? Not according to the Bible. Paul had been a believer for many years before he made this statement in Acts 24:16: "I strive always to keep my conscience clear before God and man." Paul

4

knew the value of a clear conscience and understood that work was required to keep it that way.

Parenting in a way that develops the conscience does several things. First, it helps kids know there's a right and a wrong. Not only that, it teaches them how to choose and take a stand for what's right and to wisely deal with wrongs. The conscience values integrity, so it helps children when they're tempted to be dishonest. And the conscience motivates children to think of others, and not just themselves.

The development of the conscience helps children live on two levels of thinking at the same time. Life isn't only about playing with a toy, eating food, or taking care of oneself. When teaching responsibility, every activity has a second dimension. Children learn to watch the clock, monitor their own fairness, and think about how their current action affects others. Unfortunately, some children just live on level one, thinking about the task at hand, and then rely too heavily on their parents to manage level two. Parents are continually living with level two thinking and actually become the conscience for their kids. They tell them what time it is, make sure they have their homework in their backpacks, and are quick to point out when meanness is present.

Children need to develop level two thinking in their own lives, and that can happen when parents train their children to think about more than the task at hand. Level

> The development of the conscience helps children live on two levels of thinking at the same time.

two thinking is enhanced by the work of the conscience. Kids need to always be asking questions such as, "Am I doing the right thing? Should I be helping others? Am I staying on schedule?" Even young children can begin to learn level two thinking as they consider the needs of others, clean up one activity before starting another, and learn to be grateful instead of making others miserable with their whining or complaining.

A strong conscience gives children an internal motivation to be responsible and to do the right thing even when they don't feel like it. Almost any area of parenting would benefit from a conscience approach. Parents can work with their children in a way that fosters this internal compass to help them for the rest of their lives.

God designed the conscience to keep the heart going in the right direction. The heart provides internal motivation; the conscience prompts the heart so the internal motivation stays on the right path. However, the conscience itself is only a tool. It's not the ultimate standard for right and wrong. Paul made that clear in 1 Corinthians 4:4, which says, "My conscience is clear, but that does not make me innocent. It is the Lord who judges me." A child who just got revenge might feel a temporary sense of satisfaction and an appeased conscience. That doesn't justify the actions. A person may say he feels at peace about disobedience to God. That doesn't make it right.

> God designed the conscience to keep the heart going in the right direction.

The conscience needs training. For that reason, God leaves another space in the human heart to complete the internal guidance system. The conscience is maximized by the presence of God himself living and residing inside us. First Corinthians 3:16 asks the rhetorical question, "Don't you know that you yourselves are God's temple and that God's Spirit lives in you?" When a person accepts Jesus as Lord and Savior, the Holy Spirit takes up residence inside the heart.

Some people mistakenly believe that the Holy Spirit and the conscience are the same thing. They aren't, and many of the verses in this chapter alone indicate the unique identity of each. The conscience is a human element inside every person. It's standard operating equipment for everyone, young and old. The Holy Spirit is a person who comes to live in the heart at the second birth, which the Bible calls salvation. The Holy Spirit doesn't take the place of the conscience but rather further equips it to do the work it needs to do.

The conscience and the Holy Spirit continually send messages to the heart about what's right and wrong. The conscience is a governor for the heart to keep it on track. It's only a human entity and, as a result, is imperfect. Sometimes its messages are misunderstood, misinterpreted, or simply rejected. As parents train their children, much of their work is clarifying the role and function of the conscience so their children, over time, rely less and less on Mom and Dad, and more and more on the Lord in their lives. The spiritual training described in the second section of this book is essential for healthy conscience formation and contributes greatly to level three thinking.

The third level of thinking asks the questions about God, his work in our world, and the ramifications of current actions from a spiritual perspective. Not many people get to level three thinking, but with training even young children can develop healthy patterns. Level three thinking hears about a tragedy in another country and asks questions about the Christians in that area and how the event might affect them. It's following a prompting to pray for someone when you hear about a difficult experience. As kids learn to listen to the promptings of the Holy Spirit in their lives, they often develop more spiritual sensitivity than many adults. Level three thinking takes advantage of both the conscience and the Holy Spirit to build significant maturity regarding events in life.

The challenge of conscience development is to help children become more sensitive to the inner promptings they experience, and then to have the character to evaluate those promptings and respond appropriately. If you ask a child, "Why do you do what's right?" what is the typical response? Most children will say, "So I don't get in trouble." It's then that you can take that child to Romans 13:5, which says, "It is necessary to submit to the authorities, not only because of possible punishment [external motivation] but also because of conscience [internal motivation]." Children can learn to be internally motivated, but it often takes a change in parents for that to happen.

Notice we're back to that same word again: *conscience*. The Greek word used thirty times in the New Testament for *conscience* is *syneidesis* and literally means the "self that knows." Interestingly, there is no Hebrew word for *conscience*, but the idea is certainly taught in the Old Testament, and we'll explore some of the relevant teaching as it applies to parenting.

> If you ask a child, "Why do you do what's right?" what is the typical response? Most children will say, "So I don't get in trouble."

Many children rely more on externals than they do on internals. To make the change, they need training. Sometimes kids have learned to rely on externals because of the way they're parented. A biblical study of the conscience opens the door for new, practical ways to train children.

A Common Parenting Mistake That Hinders Conscience Development

Most parents were raised on what's called "behavior modification." Ivan Pavlov discovered this system in the early 1900s as he worked with dogs. He learned that he could change the dogs' behavior and make them salivate by giving them food while ringing a bell. After several days of doing this, he would ring the bell without the food and the dogs would still salivate. Thus he trained the dogs to salivate at the sound of the bell. That may not sound too important in the broad scheme of things, but it had significant ramifications for the training of animals. Trainers have since used rewards to get animals to do all kinds of things.

In the 1920s, a man named John B. Watson started using behavior modification on people. It worked. People changed when given a reward. So it wasn't long before many new behavior modification programs became the norm. Smoking cessation systems, weight loss plans, and all kinds of learning programs used behavior modification to help people change. Soon the techniques were the model for working with children in the classroom, and then eventually in the home. Here's what it looks like in a typical home today.

Sandra is four years old. You can often hear her mom make statements like this: "Sandra, clean up your toys so you can have a snack." "Finish getting dressed so you can go out and play." Mom has learned that if she tells Sandra that she'll get a reward, Sandra is more likely to do the task. The problem is that Mom is appealing to Sandra's selfishness to get things done.

It may be easy to get a preschooler to do what you want by giving some kind of reward, but as she gets older, you have to increase the value of the reward to get the same response. You can motivate a preschooler with a quarter, but you'll need a dollar by the time she's seven, and five dollars by the time she's ten, and you'll be paying her twenty dollars at thirteen. If you continue to use the same system, by the time she's in high school, you'll have to promise her a car to get her to graduate.

The reason is clear. Behavior modification requires that you give a reward that's greater than the desire to do something different. You're simply compensating a child for doing something she'd rather not do using something she wants.

Behavior modification works because it appeals to the selfishness in a child's heart. Unfortunately, kids grow up asking the wrong questions: "What's in it for me?" and "Are you going to pay me for this?"

> Behavior modification requires that you give a reward that's greater than the desire to do something different.

Some parents label their children as strong-willed because of the battle they often experience when they try to get their children to do even the smallest of things. Parents lament, "Nothing works." They say, "He doesn't care if I take everything away; he won't change." "She doesn't care about the star chart, the trip this weekend, or dessert."

Strong-willed children know what they want and are not easily deterred. Why? Because children who are characterized as "strong-willed" already have high levels of internal motivation and are less affected by external motivations. These kids challenge the typical behavior modification system of rewards and punishment. The suggestions in this book are just the tools necessary to guide these kids in the right direction, opening up new parenting strategies for weary parents.

It's amazing how many of us have been greatly influenced by secular humanism. Parents want their children to be internally motivated, but sometimes their strategies do just the opposite. Some parents go so far as to train their children as if they're animals by inadvertently overemphasizing rewards and punishment. When that happens, parents miss the tremendous opportunities that a heart-based approach to parenting offers. In reality, parents who understand their faith realize that there's another large bucket of parenting tools that is heart-related. They help their children make progress more quickly and see them making lasting changes as well.

Children who are internally motivated tend to do things for different reasons. Instead of getting something out of their actions, they ask the question, "What's the right thing to do?" That kind of motivation comes through a different parenting approach. We call it a *heart-based approach* to parenting. It teaches internal motivation to children and takes advantage of the work of the conscience and the Holy Spirit.

Working It Out in the Correra Family

Let's go back to the morning routine in the Correra family. Dave and Anna's children are five, seven, and ten. Dave leaves for work at 7:05 a.m., and the older two kids need to be out the door by 7:45. The kids are all awake by 6:30, so they have plenty of time to get everything done, but all three of them either dawdle or get sidetracked. If Mom doesn't stay on top of them, the tension increases during the last half hour, and the morning ends unpleasantly for all.

Responsibility is always about level two thinking. The four-year-old who goes over to help a crying baby, the nine-year-old who empties the dishwasher without being asked, and the fifteen-year-old who offers to help cook dinner are all practicing responsibility by thinking about others, not just themselves. Remembering to put away toys, take out the trash, or keep the bathroom neat all require level two thinking. Children learn how to think on a second dimension when parents teach it.

For example, teaching a child to watch a clock in the morning is a lesson in responsibility. Some initial explanation and training are in order so instead of always giving the next instruction, parents are simply saying, "Watch the clock." This approach teaches children to think about level two instead of waiting for parents to instruct them. The same approach happens by pointing to the calendar or the to-do list instead of saying, "Today's the day to take the trash to the street" or micromanaging all the tasks necessary to get things ready for school the next day.

Anna and Dave called a family meeting. Together with the kids, they created a to-do list for each child of all the things that had to get done in the morning. The first one was "feet on the ground," and others included getting dressed, making the bed, eating breakfast, preparing backpacks, brushing teeth and hair, and so forth. In all, they identified nine things that each of the children needed to do.

Dad then shared a verse from the Bible to help the kids understand internal motivation. Colossians 3:23 contrasts external motivation with internal motivation: "Whatever you do, work at it with all your heart, as working for the Lord, not for men." Mom talked about what that meant for their family. She said, "When you do something with all your heart, it means that your motivation to get things done comes from inside you, not from Mom or Dad telling you what to do."

They asked each child to divide the to-do list in half, putting a few of the tasks before breakfast and a few of the tasks after breakfast. They then decided that they'd have breakfast at 6:55 a.m., with each child having completed the first part of the list. Dad, too, would get himself ready so that he could spend a few minutes with his kids in the morning before he went to work.

After breakfast, the kids would complete the rest of the tasks and be ready to go at 7:40. That gave them a five-minute "blessing time" before heading out the door. That was the time when they would congratulate one another for getting everything done and have a quick prayer for their day before the older ones headed out to the bus.

The checkpoints each morning were 6:55 and 7:40 a.m. If kids didn't meet the checkpoints, they would have to go to bed earlier in the evening. By shifting the prompters from Dad and Mom to the list and the clock, the kids were learning to manage themselves. Mom and Dad explained that they didn't want to nag anymore. They had a prayer time together and were eager to start the new program the next morning.

The first few mornings went well. As the newness wore off, however, they did some reminding, but it wasn't about the tasks. They simply announced the time occasionally to remind kids of the clock. The new plan worked well over time, and their whole family is now in a new routine. They still had to be firm at times, and some kids needed some significant correction throughout the training time, but now Dad and Mom are teaching their children to be internally motivated.

To continue the process of building internal motivation, they added one more thing to the to-do list for each person. It was called "the blessing task." Every morning each child would have to think of one more thing for the to-do list that would add to family life. It might be cleaning up the living room or bathroom, helping a younger sibling, or setting the table for dinner that evening. Mom said,

"Look at what needs to be done around here and do it without being asked. That's internal motivation."

"I'm not going to tell you what to do. You'll decide that yourself. If I told you what to do, then I'm sure you'd do it, but that would be external. I want you to think of something yourself. Look at what needs to be done around here, and do it without being asked. That's internal motivation."

13

Not only did the kids take initiative to add to family life, but they also enjoyed surprising others. Sometimes the kids needed help to think of ideas for their blessing task, and Mom would give several suggestions, but it was up to each child to choose some way to add to family life.

Building Internal Motivation

Developing internal motivation in kids is part of their training. Any area of responsibility in family life requires that people take initiative on their own. In order for children to make those kinds of changes, parents often have to adjust the way they work with their kids. As in many areas of parenting, Dave and Anna used several approaches to develop a new way of thinking for their family. Dad and Mom provided a new plan, created vision for the plan, set a measurable standard that required firmness on their part, and then the parents coached the kids to success, affirming them in the end. Instead of being the conscience for their kids, Dad and Mom parented in a way that fostered independence in their children. All of this was done with a sense of honoring God and serving him with their whole hearts.

> When parents take a heart-based approach to their parenting, they're investing in a child for the long term.

In the Correra family, they're all learning more about what it means to work as a team, get things done, and solve a significant problem, such as morning tension. The kids are learning how to become internally motivated in other areas of life as well. Sure, the process requires training, but the way Dad and Mom approach it helps their children rely on their hearts, not just on externals.

Internal motivation is a heart issue. The heart is an important target for parental training, teaching, and encouragement. Left to its own devices, the heart tends to drift from what's right. God is interested in the heart of a person, and he's provided many helpful tools to keep it moving in the right direction. The reality, however, is that most kids need training in initiative, perseverance, and moral development. It doesn't just come naturally. When parents take a heart-based approach to their parenting, they're investing in a child for the long term.

Building the Conscience Has Practical Implications Now

Maybe you're with us up to this point, willing to adjust the way you parent to embrace more moral training in your child to impact the heart. The question you're probably asking now is, "How do you do that? What can I do to help my kids?" After all, we give instructions, correct, and set limits every day. Much of our time is consumed with getting kids to where they need to be, with all the things they need when they're there, getting food on the table, and keeping the clothes cycle moving. Adding more to our already busy schedules may just put us over the edge.

Some of the suggestions we provide will add more things to your to-do list. In those cases, they're an investment in the future. For example, Dave and Anna had to make some adjustments in their morning routine. It took work to plan a new approach and practice to make it part of their family life. In the end, though, it made their morning routine easier. The work you do to develop internal motivation adds to your to-do list for a while, but in the end it relieves you of some of the tasks of micromanaging children. Your work is an investment in your future and that of your child.

On the other hand, after hearing what we have to say about building internal motivation in kids, some parents decide that they want to completely reengineer the way they work with their children. They develop new patterns, and those habits often take some time to develop. They require new communication strategies with children, new ways of coaching them to success, and even new vocabulary at times to help children develop a heightened moral awareness.

Whatever you choose to do in this area, your kids will benefit. Many children today lack the internal ability to see what needs to be done and do it, or to think about other people first instead of themselves. The following chapters will give you a greater understanding of the practical implications of moral development and how to teach it in your home.

You can start at any point. If you're picking up this book when your kids are teenagers, you're at a ripe developmental stage to teach your kids about integrity in practical ways. They'll learn how to do their best, not just the minimum to get by. They'll learn to do what they said they would do and to admit when they've made a mistake. That's integrity, a primary quality kids are developing in the teen years. As you help your teen work on integrity, you're engaged in moral development.

If you're starting when your kids are preschoolers, you can help your children by building good patterns of coming when called, following instructions, and accepting no as an answer. Many young children struggle with those things, and developing healthy patterns and practicing doing what's right can go a long way to strengthen the conscience for years to come.

As you read the next few chapters, you'll have time to evaluate your kids, learn some new ideas for teaching them, and see examples of real families who are taking steps to move in the right direction. Likely you're already doing a lot of things well.

Hopefully you'll find some new ideas of ways to enhance your work with your children. Touching the heart of a child is so important that we need all the tools and ideas we can find. We know that raising children is the toughest job in the world. It's our desire to make that job a little easier.

2

Parenting Requires Strategy

If you're too afraid to "put your foot down,"
your children will be sure to step on your toes.

This encouraging comment came to us by e-mail a few days
after one of our recent live seminars:

This biblical approach to the conscience has completely
changed the way I work with my kids. I'm surprised at how
much I relied on threats and incentives to get my kids to do
what I wanted them to do. I didn't even realize there was
another way to parent. I'm amazed at how powerful it is to
parent in a way that addresses the heart. My kids are still kids.
They still have problems, but I have a much better plan for
dealing with them than before. It's so encouraging for me to
see them move forward on their own. I see now how I am
helping them build internal motivation.

A Conscience-Based Approach
Leads to Different Strategies

These kinds of parental testimonies are a treasure for us. We work with parents every week, and we know that all families are different. Children are unique. Parents have different parenting styles and passions, but when it comes to helping children grow out of some of their most difficult problems, there's nothing that does a better job than addressing the heart and building internal motivation in kids.

Parents who incorporate the conscience into their parenting actually do things differently on a day-to-day basis. We're not just talking about having one conversation with your child about the conscience and then going on as before. New tools develop that take the place of much of the intensity that can drain a family's emotional resources.

One of the greatest strategies you can use to foster conscience development has to do with the power of your voice, because what you say and how you say it impacts your child's heart. In fact, if you think back to your own childhood, you can likely hear the words of your dad or your mom. "Turn off the lights when you leave a room." "Eat your vegetables. They're good for you." "Money just burns a hole in your pocket." One mom said, "Sometimes I'm talking to my kids and say something profound or important, and I'm shocked. I realize that I sound just like my mother."

"Brothers Love Each Other"

One mom told this story. "Our two boys are two years apart. As you might imagine, when they were young, they often competed and bickered with each other. My husband and I were determined to teach them to value their relationship together, so we began saying to them, 'Remember, brothers love each other.' We would say it when they were in conflict. We would say it when they were having fun together. We said it when they went out the door to play with friends. 'Remember, brothers love each other.' We were committed to developing a belief in their little minds about how brothers were to respond to one another. The Bible, in Romans 12:10, says, 'Be devoted to one another in brotherly love.' Our boys didn't always demonstrate love to each other as they were growing up, but they knew that loving each other was the right thing to do. Today, they're grown men and they really do love each other."

What parents say leaves a marked impression on their children's hearts. Unfortunately, many parents spend too much time talking about what children are doing wrong and not what they need to do right instead. They say things like, "Would you cut it out!" "Stop it!" "When are you going to get it right?" "You're making me upset here." "I can't believe you keep doing this."

> What parents say leaves a marked impression on their children's hearts.

Rather, parents would do much better thinking about what they want their children to say in their hearts, and then using their own statements to their children to coach them to that end. One dad told of his challenge with his son who has attention deficit/hyperactivity disorder. As you might imagine, these children can be magnets for correction. Dad realized that his words to his son were strategic as he coached him in life every day, many times a day. He and his wife developed a list of things they would say to their son to help him stay on track. The list was made up of statements they wanted him to say to himself, and included things such as, "Slow motion." "Quiet voice." "Think before you speak." "Maybe you need to take a break." "Manage your energy." Their approach provided a positive way to keep their son moving toward the goal of developing self-control in his life.

The Bible reveals that people meditate on things in their hearts. Psalm 19:14 says, "May the words of my mouth and the meditation of my heart be pleasing in your sight, O LORD, my Rock and my Redeemer." Notice where the meditation takes place—in the heart. When parents choose their words carefully, they're contributing to the right kind of meditation for their children. Too many kids say unhelpful things in their hearts. Parents can write the script of things that are more appropriate. As moms and dads correct, instruct, remind, and coach their children throughout the day, they can go back to the predetermined list and use it for ideas of what to say.

> When parents choose their words carefully, they're contributing to the right kind of meditation for their children.

Writing the script for your children molds their thinking and helps develop the right beliefs in their hearts. It's one of the significant ways that parents can influence what children believe about life. The conscience is on a hunt for right and wrong, looking for promptings to provide to the heart. A parent's words often become those promptings for a child as he or she remembers the words of Mom or Dad when faced with various life situations.

Tone of Voice Makes a Strong Statement

But it's not just the words parents use that impact conscience development. It's also the way they say them. One mom told this story: "My two young boys went out to play Wiffle ball in the backyard. I thought it was so cute that I decided to video record the fun. I held the camera as I supervised their play, and then we went into the house to watch the video. I was surprised by the tone of my voice in the background of the video. It had a harshness I didn't realize. I determined at that point that I would change the way I talk to my kids and become more gracious in my speech. It wasn't what I said, but how I said it that caused me to feel uncomfortable."

Many of us don't hear our own tone of voice. We may hear a tone we don't like in a mate or in a teenager, but it's harder to hear in ourselves. The underlying message children hear when we become harsh or intense may be unproductive. When kids receive harshness from their parents, they often go away from the experience hearing, "I'm unworthy," "I'm unloved," or "I'm not valuable." That's certainly not the intent of the parent, but that's often what children perceive and remember when an unhelpful tone is allowed to creep into our conversation. Those same feelings can appear at unwanted times in a child's life if the conscience is sending out unhelpful messages to the child, learned from continual comments from the parent.

Of course, over time, some children begin to tune out their parents' words, especially harsh or angry ones. It's wise to be encouraging and nurturing with tone and content so that kids receive a regular message that relationship is important and their parents may have something valuable to say.

Choosing Words Carefully

Parents communicate significant messages to their children every day. The mom at the park who says twenty times in two minutes, "Be careful," is communicating a message that safety is of supreme importance. Is that the message you want your child to hear? Some kids need that message over and over again, but others need a completely different message. Some kids are afraid to step out and try something new, and their parents may contribute to the problem by saying, "Be careful" too much. Maybe those children need a different message that says, "Go ahead, you can do it" or "I like it that you try new things." Imagine how those parental promptings affect a child's internal promptings over time. Inadvertently, those parents are training the child's conscience to provide promptings of the value of safety or the value of taking risks, both significant messages children need to hear.

> Some kids are afraid to step out and try something new, and their parents may contribute to the problem by saying, "Be careful" too much.

Children believe things in their hearts, and much of what they believe comes from what their parents tell them. Fred and Lynn saw a problem in their daughter, Shannon. They realized that she didn't work hard. When given a task to do at school, at home, or even by a friend, Shannon looked for ways to opt out. As the parents evaluated the situation, they realized that Shannon believed something wrong about life. She believed that her job description in life was to have fun. As Fred and Lynn further considered the problem, they realized that they may have contributed to this misbelief. When their daughter left the house, they would often send her out by saying, "Have fun." Shannon seemed to believe that having fun was her mission in life. Furthermore, when Shannon came back and they were debriefing about the day, Fred and Lynn would often ask the question, "Did you have fun?" They realized that was not the question they wanted to ask, so they determined to do things differently.

These parents began saying different things to their daughter on her way out the door, such as, "Do the right thing" and

"Take care of your brother." Of course, Fred and Lynn needed to implement some other strategies to teach Shannon to work hard, but considering the words they used was an important part of their strategy.

What's the message a mother gives to her children when she says, "You'll be in trouble when your dad gets home"? Maybe kids begin to believe that Mom doesn't have the authority or strength to discipline. Or when Dad calls out to his five-year-old, "You better come now, or I'll leave you here," a child may believe that the reason to respond to Dad's authority is so he doesn't get left behind. Of course, the real reason he should come is because it's the right thing to do.

Children believe things in their hearts, and parents contribute to that thinking, both good and bad. When you take time to evaluate the things you say to your child, you can become more strategic in your parenting. There's no doubt that parental words are important. Proverbs 1:8 says, "Listen, my son, to your father's instruction and do not forsake your mother's teaching." That's one of eleven times in the book of Proverbs that God tells children to listen to their moms and dads. Why? Because parents have something to say. That means that parents need to choose what they say carefully, because their words, and how they say them, impact their kids' hearts.

Action Point

Another area where the power of a parent's voice is revealed takes place when parents give instructions. When parents give multiple warnings or instructions without requiring immediate action, children learn to put up with those promptings and delay the action until they know that the action is required, often demonstrated by an emotional cue of anger by the parent.

In some homes parents talk and talk and talk and talk and then explode before a child does what's been asked. This common problem reveals a need to tighten one's "action point." An action point is the point where you, as a parent, stop talking and start acting. Your action indicates that your words are important.

Every adult who works with children has an action point, and children know what it is. Dad may get the kids moving faster than Mom. The babysitter may not have a very tight action point. Children may respond better to instructions at school, and when you seek to discover why, you come back to the way the teacher gives instructions. It reveals a clear action point.

> Every adult who works with children has an action point, and children know what it is.

Think for a moment about how your children know when you mean business. If you don't know, you might ask them. In some families, a parent uses the child's middle name. Other times you might start moving toward the child. Or you might start moving to the kitchen where that special utensil is. Kids know you mean business, and they start obeying. In many homes, the action point is demonstrated by anger. Take Sammy, for example.

Sammy is five and is playing with his toys on the floor in the living room. Mom decides it's time to go do some errands, so she says, "Sammy, get your shoes on. We're going to go do some errands." Mom then goes around the house, getting herself ready. When she comes back a couple of minutes later, Sammy doesn't have his shoes on. "Sammy, get your shoes on. We're going to do some errands." Then Mom continues around the house, cleaning up a couple more things so she can be ready to go. As she passes back through the living room, she sees that Sammy hasn't started to get ready.

To make the instruction sound more important, she starts giving reasons. "Sammy, we have to go to the store, stop by the school, and drop these books off at the library. Go get your shoes on so we can leave." Mom goes back to getting her things together that she needs for the trip and comes back a couple of minutes later to find that Sammy hasn't moved at all. Now she's angry. She bursts into the room and yells, "Sammy!" and Sammy gets up and gets his shoes on.

Now imagine the same scenario from Sammy's perspective. He's enjoying his toys and hears Mom the first time and thinks, *It sounds like Mom is talking in the other room.* He continues to play with his toys. Mom comes in a couple of minutes later and he says to himself, *I think we're going somewhere today.* He continues to play with his toys. Mom comes in again and he thinks, *It's getting closer.* When Mom finally bursts into the room with anger, he realizes, *Oh, it's time to go,* and he gets up and gets his shoes on.

Most children, like Sammy, know what the action point is, and they know they don't have to get moving until they see it. To increase the power of your words, you'll want to tighten your action point so your words have weight in your child's mind. Some parents identify with this little story and say, "But my kids won't get moving unless I get angry." If that's the case, it's because you've trained them that way. As you tighten your action point, your children will have to change.

Evaluating Parental Cues

Children respond to parental cues, and they can learn to respond to different ones if you teach them. Instead of using emotional cues to indicate when you mean business, we would suggest you use word cues instead. Children need to understand the difference between an idea, an opinion, a question, and an instruction.

If you want to get your daughter in bed, you don't say, "Would you like to go to bed now?" If you want your son to work on his homework, you don't say, "I think you should work on your homework now." That's an opinion, and your son may have a different opinion.

It's not wrong to share opinions or ideas with your kids, but you want your *instructions* to sound different. Sometimes parents, knowing they will get resistance, try to sugarcoat their words of instruction to sound more gracious, but most children don't then hear it like an instruction. They just perceive it as some kind of idea. You don't need intensity or harshness, but you do need to be clear.

> It's not wrong to share opinions or ideas with your kids, but you want your *instructions* to sound different.

We would suggest you use word cues that communicate, "What I'm about to say to you is something I expect you to do right away." You might start with the child's name, end with the word *now*, and say, "You need to," somewhere in the middle. For example, you might say, "Sammy, you need to get your shoes on now." That's a clear instruction. It sounds different from other dialogue you have with your child, and you've clarified for your child that this is an instruction and that you mean it.

But talk is not enough. An action point requires action. You might say, "What if I tell Sammy to get his shoes on with that special wording and he still sits there?" That's a good question. It's not words alone that initiate change. It's action associated with those words that communicates that you mean what you say. To train Sammy, you're going to have to take some action immediately when he doesn't respond. There are lots of good ways to train him in this area. You could, for example, go to your toolbox of consequences. But parents often move to consequences too quickly. Although consequences are good, there are only a limited number of them. If you use them continually to produce action in your kids, then they tend to wear out and lose some of their effectiveness.

Applying a Conscience Approach

Let's use a conscience approach in this situation to train Sammy. He doesn't yet feel uncomfortable when given an instruction. One of the signs of responsibility is to complete assignments without the need for prodding or reminding. Responsibility is associated with an uncomfortable feeling inside a person's heart when given a task. That uncomfortable feeling motivates a person to action. We're not saying that the child feels uncomfortable with the parent, but rather that the child feels a sense of obligation because a task has been given and isn't yet done. It's the conscience that produces that uncomfortable feeling.

Mom typically responds to Sammy's lack of movement by yelling and threatening him. She threatens to take away his toys, send him to bed early, or anything else that comes to mind. Sometimes she even follows through, but Sammy still isn't changing his pattern. Mom then looks to parenting books to find more consequences she can use on her son to get him to change. Consequences aren't the solution. The problem has to do with the interaction between Sammy and Mom.

Mom needs to make a change. In fact, many times parents have to change the way they parent before kids change the way they live. Mom may sit down with Sammy and clarify the change she's going to make. "Sammy, I've noticed that when I give you an instruction, you tend to wait and not obey right away. In fact, it looks like you wait until I get angry before you start moving. I know you don't like it when I get angry, and I don't like it either, so we're going to make a change. I think I've been in the habit of starting to tell you way in advance and nagging you to get going. I'm not going to do that anymore. Instead, I'll give you a five-minute warning when I can, but then when I say, 'It's time to go,' you need to get up and go right away."

Having a positive meeting with Sammy is only the first step. Next, Mom needs to demonstrate change with her actions. When she gives Sammy an instruction, she waits there to see if he starts moving. If not, she may go over to him, get close, and say, "Sammy, you're not obeying me. You need to get up now." The close proximity raises the felt value of the instruction, and Mom's presence makes Sammy feel uncomfortable. It's not wrong for Mom to give her son notice that they're leaving to go do errands, but when she's ready to give the instruction, she must be ready to follow through immediately, thus tightening her action point.

Over time, by creating discomfort, Mom will train Sammy to realize that when given an instruction, he needs to take action and not delay. Mom is not only training Sammy to respond to instructions, but she's also training Sammy's conscience to prompt him to feel uncomfortable when he's been given an instruction. Mom may still have to use a consequence, but she'll tighten up her point of action so that Sammy recognizes the importance of an instruction.

It's not the consequence that will eventually change Sammy's heart. It's the continual practice of associating an instruction with an uncomfortable feeling that produces conscience development. Over time, Sammy will develop an internal motivation to do the right thing without delay because of the benefits of a clear conscience.

Imagine Sammy now at fifteen. He's playing his video game. He gets an internal prompter that says, *I should be working on my homework.* If, for the last ten years, he's been used to putting Mom's promptings off, then he just says to himself, *No, I can do it later.* He continues this internal dialogue until he gets to a crisis stage, and then takes action. However, if he's learned to respond to the promptings of his mother over the years, the conscience now prompts him to take action, and he's more likely to have the character to respond and do what's right.

A Tight Action Point Builds Internal Character

The idea of tightening your action point can benefit children of all ages. Some parents shy away to give their kids space, thinking they're doing their children a favor. What children often need is more parenting, not more space, so they can develop the internal responses necessary for developing responsibility and an internal commitment to do what's right.

A tight action point helps develop character so children have the self-discipline necessary to respond to the conscience as they grow and develop instead of postponing things that need to get done. Procrastination is diminished in anyone's life with a sensitive conscience and strong character. Both can develop in a child's heart through training.

> Procrastination is diminished in anyone's life with a sensitive conscience and strong character.

There are two indicators that point to the need to tighten your action point. One is anger and the other is nagging. If you're engaged in either of those two things in the instruction process, then likely the solution is to tighten your action point.

A parent's words are important in a child's life. They linger in the heart and become food for the conscience. Although the conscience isn't the ultimate authority in a person's life, it is a tool that helps keep the heart moving in the right direction. It needs training and is only as reliable as it is nurtured and equipped. Parents contribute to conscience development by carefully choosing their words and teaching their children that their words have value.

3

What Is the Conscience?

One of the greatest things you can do
for a child is to help him strengthen the
conscience. As you do, it will become a
powerful force to guide him through life.

Kara was frustrated with her nine-year-old daughter, Cassy, and as she listened to us teach about the conscience, she was encouraged by its practical approach, but still had some questions. "Sometimes Cassy needs continual prompting. She doesn't seem to be aware of things unless I tell her what to do. And other times it seems as if her conscience is overactive. For example, she is a people pleaser. She seems more eager to please people than to do what's right. How can I apply these ideas to her life?"

Kara was on the right track but needed more information about what the conscience does and how it operates so she could develop a specific strategy for her daughter. Whether your child is a preschooler, in elementary school, or a teenager, a deeper understanding of the conscience can increase his or her internal motivation.

The conscience gives four promptings. Each one provides that uncomfortable feeling in the heart that motivates a person to take action. They are: *do what's right, deal with wrongs, be honest,* and *care about others.* In this chapter we'll help you understand the biblical basis for them, and then the following chapters will give you practical ideas for parenting in a way that develops a strong conscience in those four areas in a child's heart.

> The conscience gives four promptings: do what's right, deal with wrongs, be honest, and care about others.

The conscience, although an imperfect indicator, helps us feel comfortable when we're doing what's right and uncomfortable when doing the wrong thing. The Bible indicates that the conscience prompts a person in four ways. Each one is outlined here, with its biblical basis. We helped Kara see specific ways that the conscience was working and not working in her daughter.

Do What's Right

One sign of maturity in children of any age is a growing sense of internal obligation to manage oneself. That sense of obligation is the prompting of the conscience. The three-year-old who puts his toy away before getting another, the seven-year-old who gets herself ready in the morning without being told to do so, and the fourteen-year-old who takes the trash down to the street on trash day without being reminded all bring joy to their parents' hearts. Parents feel admiration and gratefulness that their kids are growing up.

A function of the conscience is to prompt a child to do what's right. In one home Grandpa was impressed that his five-year-old grandson took his plate, cup, and silverware off the table without being asked at the end of the meal. When Grandpa started to leave the table, the young boy reminded him that he needed to do the same. That sense of obligation came as a result of training by Dad and Mom over several weeks, but now their son knew what was right in their family, and he was able to do it without being reminded. The child had developed an internal motivation to do what's right, prompted by the conscience.

When Paul the apostle was brought before the Sanhedrin to account for his actions, he used the word *conscience* in this statement in Acts 23:1, "My brothers, I have fulfilled my duty to God in all good conscience to this day." Paul tied the word *conscience* to *fulfilling his duty*. The conscience creates an internal sense of obligation and makes a person feel uncomfortable with a task that's incomplete and comfortable when that task is done.

Just think of your own personal to-do list. Whether you write it down or not, it's still on your heart and weighs on you until you take time to get those things done. Some people like to cross the last thing off the list before they throw the paper into the trash. Why do they do that? There's a sense of satisfaction when tasks are complete and obligations are satisfied.

This part of the conscience prompts a child internally to be thorough with chores, abide by family rules when with friends, and take a stand for righteousness when confronted with temptation. Kara realized that Cassy would benefit from some work in this area of the conscience because it helps produce responsibility and maturity.

Sometimes the conscience produces a feeling of discomfort regarding moral areas, such as returning a lost wallet to its rightful owner or telling the truth, but other times it's not particularly a moral issue. It's just a sense of responsibility. A four-year-old sees the light on in the bathroom and turns it off without prompting.

A ten-year-old hears the heat come on in the house and recognizes that the windows are open, and feels uncomfortable enough to get up and report it to Mom. When a fifteen-year-old sees the trash overflowing and takes it out, that's the conscience at work. Whether the discomfort produced from the conscience is moral or practical, it still gives an indicator that something is wrong and that the child should take some action.

Deal with Wrongs

The Old Testament tells a beautiful story about a woman named Abigail. She realized that David was about to do something he would regret. Her husband, Nabal, had mistreated David, and David had determined to kill Nabal and all his men. He mustered his army and was on his way to get revenge. That's when Abigail came on the scene.

Bowing down in the ravine, she stopped David in his tracks and made an effective appeal to him. "The LORD will certainly make a lasting dynasty for my master," she told him. Then she begged him not to commit the wrongdoing he had planned, because then he would "not have on his conscience the staggering burden of needless bloodshed or of having avenged himself" (1 Samuel 25: 28, 30).

Abigail appealed to David's conscience, and it worked. David turned around and went back home because she had given him a preview of what happens when you do the wrong thing. It creates a weight in one's life. She called it a "staggering burden." We all know what it's like to experience the internal weight of having done the wrong thing. A proper understanding of the conscience is very significant in this area.

The emotion that prompts a person to avoid wrongs or deal with them after the fact is *guilt*. Some people today teach that guilt is a bad thing and that one should ignore the feeling and try to move on. But God created the heart to be sensitive to wrongs, and guilt is actually a good emotion prompting a person toward repentance and reconciliation. The internal prompting is already there for kids, and they need to learn how to respond to it properly in order to be inter-nally motivated to handle mistakes and offenses well.

> The emotion that prompts a person to avoid wrongs or deal with them after the fact is *guilt*.

Unfortunately, many children don't understand the value of guilt. Instead, they try to avoid it by blaming problems on others. They rationalize, justify, or defend themselves when corrected. Most children need help in this area, and a conscience-based approach by parents will contribute to their maturity. We have much to say about this area of the conscience and have developed several tools for helping parents work with their children. Some kids react with anger when corrected and verbally attack their parents or others. The child who tends to be a perfectionist gets angry with himself and often comes to unhelpful conclusions about self-worth because of mistakes made. Most children misunder-stand correction and take offense with discipline. All that can change with good training, and parents can do several things to enhance their kids' internal motivation to handle offenses.

Kara was pleased to report that her daughter seemed to do pretty well in this area of the conscience. When Cassy was wrong, she would admit it.

Be Honest

Romans 9:1 says, "I speak the truth in Christ—I am not lying, my *conscience* confirms it in the Holy Spirit." Paul connected speaking the truth and not lying to an internal prompter, the conscience. We all know that feeling of misleading someone and feeling bad about it. The conscience prompts us with an internal desire to have integrity. Some kids have a significant problem in this area. Sometimes the problem is lying, but other forms of dishonesty may include stealing, cheating, or being mischievous or sneaky. Still other children exaggerate stories or make themselves the hero as they retell an event. Those children need help knowing how to have integrity in their lives. Many times the temptation to be dishonest is greater than a child's character. Parental training can do a lot to help kids develop integrity on a personal level.

It's disheartening for parents when they see dishonesty in their children's lives. Since honesty is foundational to human relationships, lying or stealing cuts right to the heart and damages underlying trust. It's critical that parents teach their children how to manage the truth in difficult situations. Since dishonesty generally occurs under pressure, kids need to have the internal strength to face the temptation to cut corners, be sneaky, or color the truth.

> Since honesty is foundational to human relationships, lying or stealing cuts right to the heart and damages underlying trust.

Learning how to handle the truth in life situations isn't as easy as it sounds. Children regularly find themselves in awkward situations where they must respond. How do you react when someone asks your opinion and you don't want to hurt that person with the truth? What do you say when challenged by a question where you don't feel it's appropriate to respond by telling the truth? Those are real questions, and children need to learn how to handle them.

At the same time, children often have desires that lead them into temptation to use dishonest means to get what they want or to avoid a consequence. That's a character issue and must be addressed with some practical integrity training. Although Cassy wouldn't outright lie, it seemed that sometimes she would exaggerate stories with her friends to motivate them to appreciate her more. This was definitely a temptation that needed to be addressed, and Kara was interested in understanding this part of the conscience some more.

Care About Others

The fourth area of the conscience focuses on others and is prompted by an internal emotion we call *compassion*. We like to tell the following story to children:

When Jesus was leaving Jericho, two blind men yelled from the side of the road, "Son of David, have mercy on us!" (Matthew 20:31). The Bible tells us that the crowd rebuked the men, but Jesus had compassion on them and healed them. What's the difference between the crowd and Jesus? The crowd was thinking of themselves, interested in their parade and not wanting to be bothered. Jesus was different. He stopped and helped the men. The Bible says that he had something inside that prompted him to do that. It's the same thing you and I can have in our lives to help us to think of others and not just ourselves. "Jesus had compassion" (v. 24).

Compassion is more than just a feeling. Empathy is the underlying feeling, but compassion results in action. Some children are naturally compassionate, thinking of the needs of others and trying to help them or relieve their frustration or pain. Other kids need help in this area. The good news is that every child can learn to be compassionate, even if they have a tendency to be self-focused. It's not just a personality trait. All kids need to develop compassion and the ability to care about others.

When someone is hurt, struggling, or frustrated, the person with a strong conscience has an internal motivation to help. The conscience provides sensitivity to another person's emotions and then prompts action. Of course, wisdom is required for a child to know how and when to respond to a need. Parents can help strengthen this area of the conscience by focusing on it in their training.

Nathan the prophet used this area of the conscience of caring about others to reveal David's sin. He told him a story of a man whose only lamb was taken for food by a man who had plenty of his own sheep. David felt the unfairness and was incensed by the mistreatment. His compassion resulted in immediate action, the decision to find the guilty party and punish him. Nathan then revealed that David himself was the guilty party, having stolen another man's wife. David was cut to the heart, conscience stricken, and convicted by God for his sin (2 Samuel 12:13).

In Luke 10, a man asked Jesus, "What must I do to inherit eternal life?" "What is written in the Law?" he replied. "How do you read it?" Jesus affirmed the man's answer that he must first love God and then love his neighbor as himself. Here's where the story takes an interesting turn. The next verse says that the man sought to justify himself by asking, "Who is my neighbor?" (vv. 25–29). The fact that he was seeking to justify himself is a statement of the man's attempt to satisfy his conscience. In essence, he was saying, "What's the minimum I need to do in order to fulfill the command to care about others?"

Jesus answered by telling the famous story of the good Samaritan, an illustration of a man who went out of his way to care for a man in need. Jesus then asked the man, "Which of the three men in the story was the neighbor?" The man said, "The one who had mercy on him." Jesus was teaching that each person has a responsibility to care for others, not just themselves, an important message that children need and can learn.

This was definitely the area where Cassy needed some work. It wasn't that she was weak in this area, but she seemed to be overly sensitive to others' opinions. Her desire to think about others needed balance. As we continued to help Kara with her daughter, we focused on convictions and doing what's right, two very important conscience principles. She also helped her daughter evaluate the promptings she had on the inside. Sometimes those promptings were good, and other times they came from internal desires to be liked or valued. Although that isn't always wrong, it's certainly dangerous, often tempting a person to compromise integrity.

Raising the Awareness Level

Some children are stronger in one area of the conscience than in others. For example, one child may not have a problem with lying at all, but is also rather self-focused and uncaring about others. Other children have a hard time receiving correction and dealing with wrongs, but they have caring hearts. The good news is that often you can use areas of strength in a child's life to help him or her improve areas of weakness. As Kara talked about the conscience with Cassy, she saw that her daughter's awareness level was increasing. She was learning more about those internal prompters she was already experiencing.

Some children are stronger in one area of the conscience than in others.

One mom reported a conversation with her teenage son that

went like this: "I notice that you have a sensitivity to the feelings of others. I really like that. You look for ways to help when you see that someone feels bad. That's a sign of a strong conscience in the area of caring about others. However, there's another area of the conscience I think you'll want to be working on, and I'll look for ways to help you. You seem to struggle with doing a complete job and reporting back when you're done. That's the area of the conscience we call 'doing the right thing.' It would be helpful if you could take some of that uncomfortable feeling you experience when others are sad and bring it into this area of doing a job thoroughly.

"A responsible person feels the same discomfort when a job isn't completed well. You may want to think about that some more, because I can tell that you have what it takes to use your conscience for good. It may be helpful for you to think about how incomplete chores affect others. That may help you be more thoughtful about doing a good job. Understanding how the conscience is working in your heart is just another area that will help you be strong on the inside."

Internal motivation develops when parents focus on the heart instead of simply using reward and punishment to get their kids to act.

It's interesting how many issues in family life are touched by the four promptings of the conscience. The kids who are bickering with each other can learn compassion and care for each other instead of putting each other down. The child who doesn't finish homework or who tends to be lazy needs greater work in the area of doing what's right. When a child won't take responsibility for a mistake or sin, that's a conscience issue. Working on the conscience in children is not only a biblical approach, but it's also very practical. Internal motivation develops in children when parents focus on the heart instead of simply using reward and punishment to get their kids to act.

You may want to take some time to think about the areas where your child struggles, and then ask yourself what part of the conscience can help with that area of weakness. Of course, you'll find some overlap between the areas of the conscience, but thinking in these terms can give you direction as you develop a strategy to move forward. Here's a report card to help you evaluate areas of strength and weakness in your child's conscience.

Already Strong	Needs Improvement	Do What's Right
○	○	My child does what I say without resistance.
○	○	My child completes a job instead of doing it partway.
○	○	My child does what's right even when no one is around to watch.
○	○	My child is able to stand against peer pressure.
○	○	My child works hard to complete a job that's difficult.
○	○	My child takes a stand for what's right.
○	○	My child reports back when a job is completed.
○	○	....
○	○	....

Already Strong	Needs Improvement	
		## Deal with Wrongs
○	○	My child admits when he's done the wrong thing.
○	○	My child responds well to correction.
○	○	My child values correction and learns from it.
○	○	My child accepts responsibility for his part of the problem.
○	○	My child feels remorse for an offense.
○	○	My child takes initiative to make wrongs right.
○	○	My child feels uncomfortable with wrong and seeks to avoid it.
○	○	....
○	○	....
		## Be Honest
○	○	My child tells the truth.
○	○	My child is honest when no one is watching.
○	○	My child avoids stealing, cheating, and lying.
○	○	My child speaks honestly when confronted with an offense.
○	○	My child takes a stand for integrity when faced with dishonest options.
○	○	My child tells a story without exaggerating or embellishing it.
○	○	....
○	○	....

Already Strong	Needs Improvement	**Care About Others**
○	○	My child thinks about the feelings of others.
○	○	My child is kind to siblings, friends, and others.
○	○	My child is on the lookout to help people.
○	○	My child cleans up his messes and contributes to the cleanup of others too.
○	○	My child looks for things that need to be done and does them.
○	○	My child wants to make the world a better place.
○	○	....
○	○	....

4

Helping Kids Choose to Do What's Right

Responsibility is doing what you know you
should do, even when you don't want to.

B ob is four years old and regularly leaves his pajamas on the
floor in the bedroom after he gets dressed. Mom wants to
help him manage himself in this simple area. How can she use
a conscience approach to help her son do what's right without
being told?

All parents want to help their children develop responsibility, and it happens at any age. A three-year-old puts away his toys,
an eight-year-old cleans up the counter after getting a drink, a
thirteen-year-old cleans up the bathroom without being asked,
and an eighteen-year-old checks in and abides by a curfew.
These are all signs of internal motivation and demonstrations
of responsibility. They reveal that the conscience is growing and
motivating the child in life. Responsibility develops as children
learn to rely on the internal prompting to do what's right. That's

one of the four promptings of the conscience and the one we'll focus on in this chapter.

Building a Sense of Obligation

Responsibility training requires transferring ownership to the child, not just to complete a task, but to do it well, and to remember to get it done. A strong conscience keeps a child on track when tempted to play instead of work, do a minimal job, or forget the job altogether. Parents can do several things to strengthen the conscience and help build responsibility. The goal is to help children feel an internal obligation to complete the task instead of relying on parents, teachers, or others to be those prompters.

> The goal is to help children feel an internal obligation to complete the task instead of relying on parents, teachers, or others to be those prompters.

Being responsible, organized, and reliable requires that children be sensitive to internal cues. Often internal cues are attached to external indicators, such as a calendar, a clock, or a to-do list. Just think about yourself for a moment. How do you remember when to get the oil changed in the car, when it's time to buy more toilet paper, or to send a card to your mother on her birthday? You typically have indicators you use to remind you to get those things done. You may watch the mileage on the car and know when the next oil change is needed. When you open the last package of toilet paper, that's your indication that you need to put it on the shopping list, and you might put a reminder on your calendar for important birthdays. Those indicators keep you self-motivated.

In addition, you rely on cues that remind you to take needed action. When the grass gets high, you mow the lawn. When the dog starts whining, you take him out for a walk. When the trash gets full, you take it out. Children can also learn to see cues, feel uncomfortable about the situation, and do something about it. Your children can learn to do the same thing you do, but it will take some thought, creativity, and practice.

If Mom asks Bob to go in and put his pajamas away, he'll do it. He was not being disobedient, he just didn't think to do it on his own. Mom decides to set up a plan to help Bob be more responsible about his pajamas. She meets with Bob and says something like this: "Bob, you're four years old now, and you're growing up fast. I like how grown up you act. But I see one thing I think would be helpful for us to work on. I notice that every day when you get dressed, you leave your pajamas on the floor. What should you be doing instead?"

"Putting them back in the drawer," says Bob.

"That's right. I know you just forget, but one of the signs of growing up is that you learn to remember on your own. I'd like to work on that with you to help you take care of this yourself. Make sense?"

"Yes, but I forget."

"I understand. I forget things too. So we have to set up a way for you to remember. Here's my idea. Every day, before you leave your room, as you touch the doorknob to open the door, I'd like you to ask yourself the question, 'Did I finish the job?' That will remind you to look around in your room to see if it's ready for you to leave it. What do you think of that?"

"Okay, but I still might forget."

"I know. So I thought it might be good for you to create some kind of reminder on your doorknob to help you remember. Why don't you think of an idea and let me know what this reminder is going to look like."

Bob may choose to tie on a piece of red yarn or create a little picture sign. The parental work is not over, but now it changes so that the focus transitions to building internal motivation inside Bob. Mom no longer reminds Bob to put away his pajamas.

> Mom no longer reminds Bob to put away his pajamas. Now she says, "Doorknob" or "Red yarn."

Now she says, "Doorknob" or "Red yarn." Mom works to connect the indicator to the conscience so that Bob remembers to be responsible with his pajamas. In most cases, by transferring the cues to the child in this way, children begin to learn responsibility in specific tasks. That doesn't mean instant change. Sometimes Bob may not feel like putting his pajamas away or may be so excited that he doesn't stop to think. But the way Mom is now parenting transfers her directives to an internal system of reminding instead of simply being the reminder system for her son. She's equipping and strengthening the conscience in her son.

Holding Kids Accountable to Their Own Plans

The desire to postpone tasks is a common one and works against responsibility. If you're working with a teenager, you might give the task of cleaning up the kitchen. Your daughter may delay and delay, and the job may not get done. You can step in to be the parental prompter and keep her on track, but let's try a conscience approach to address this problem. You might say something like this: "Melinda, your job is to clean up the kitchen this evening. I don't want to be nagging you about it, so why don't you tell me your plan, and then I'll feel okay because I know that you're on top of things and not just delaying indefinitely."

"I'll get it done before I go to bed."

"I'm sorry. That plan isn't going to work. I want to go to bed at 10:00 p.m., and I'd like to see that kitchen done earlier than that so I can check it."

"Okay. I'll do it by 8:00 p.m."

"Great. Thank you. I'm okay with that."

Then you leave and go about your business. If at 8:00 p.m. your daughter hasn't even started the kitchen, you're back. "You told me you'd work on the kitchen by 8:00 p.m."

"I'll do it in a bit."

"No, you need to get up now and start working on it."

After your daughter completes the kitchen and you check her work, you might then say, "I want to give you some freedom to help decide your schedule, but if you can't do what you said you will do, then you'll lose the privilege of deciding when you'll do it. If you give me a plan and stick to it, you're demonstrating integrity by doing what you said you would do. That's a sign of maturity. If you don't do what you say, then you're going to lose the privilege of helping determine when you're going to do the job."

If the problem persists, then, as a parent, you may have to require that she clean up the kitchen immediately after dinner, with the understanding that if she does it with a good attitude, you may allow her to help determine the schedule next time. It has to do with being reliable. This kind of an approach, used over time, helps children feel uncomfortable when they've agreed to do something until it gets done. That's helping to strengthen the conscience.

Asking teens, "What's your plan?" instead of barging in and demanding instant obedience can be a way of teaching them to be responsible. It passes the responsibility on to the child to help determine details and to remember to get things done. Notice that the parent isn't absent from the process, but instead looks for ways to change from being the conscience to developing the conscience in the child.

Thinking on Two Levels

Responsibility requires that a person think on two levels at the same time. One has to do with the task at hand, and the other has to do with quality of work, time schedule, organization, and the expectations of others. For example, Chase is playing a video game. If he is responsible, then he can enjoy the game but also set limits on his actions. He's conscious of his brother waiting for a turn, homework that needs to get done, and the time limits his parents have set for video games. On one level he's enjoying the game, while on another level he's conscious of other tasks and issues, takes them into account, and adjusts his game playing accordingly. That's responsibility and demonstrates a sensitivity to the promptings of the conscience.

Most children don't think on the second level, and many aren't even aware that it exists. In fact, many kids rely on parents to think on that second level for them. Parents who take on this role instead of teaching their kids to do it for themselves are continually prompting their children to remember the time, other tasks that must get done, and how their behavior is affecting others. Many parents who realize that they have taken over the second-level thinking for their kids also see that they have become the conscience for their children and recognize the need to make some changes.

For example, Chase is weak in the responsibility area, and his parents want to raise his awareness of the second level for him. Dad explains the new plan this way: "Chase, I see that you enjoy your video game. There's nothing wrong with that. Video games can be fun. But playing games is a problem when other things don't get done. Being aware of other things and adjusting your actions to take care of them are demonstrations of responsibility. For example, if you keep playing and don't allow your brother a turn, then you're allowing the first level, enjoying the game, to hinder the second level, your obligation to your brother. Limiting level one, playing the game, to take care of other things on level two, like homework and staying within our designated time for video games, demonstrates responsibility.

"We're going to set up a system to help you focus more on level two kinds of things. Here's the plan. During your video game playing, every fifteen minutes you need to report to me. You have one minute of time during which you need to say, 'Dad, I'm checking in.' If you remember, then it means that while you're playing, you're also watching the clock, one of the signs of responsibility. Checking in allows you to play for fifteen more minutes. If, however, you become so attached to the game that you can't watch the clock, then you'll miss the next fifteen minutes of playing time."

Now Chase is learning to be internally motivated to do what's right and to think outside of his current action to other things that are also important.

Watching the clock is just one of the signs of a responsible person. Tying video game playing to watching the clock helps a child become more conscious of two levels of life. The second level focuses on responsibility. These parents are helping Chase build self-management skills by transferring the responsibility to the child.

As a side note, to be discussed later, there's a level three kind of thinking that focuses on the spiritual, what God is doing and how he wants a person to live. Children who learn to move from level one thinking to levels two and three thinking maximize their perception of life.

Developing Convictions

As we've already pointed out, the conscience is not designed to be one's authority in life. Some children feel comfortable or uncomfortable in inappropriate ways and may get false indicators from an untrained conscience. When Ramón punches his sister and then feels satisfied that he's gotten revenge, he's mistaken and needs some training. Just because someone feels a sense of peace about something, it doesn't make it right. When Joseph makes a mistake, he internalizes the guilt and says a number of bad things to himself, such as, "I'm an idiot. I'm never going to get it right." Understanding the conscience and responding well to it requires training.

The conscience doesn't work alone. It looks for a standard upon which to rely. If a person isn't a Christian, then the standard for life is the greatest good he or she can imagine. However, Christians realize that God gave us the Bible to be our standard, and believers rely on God's Word for their lives. A trained conscience feeds off of the Scriptures. Not all actions have a Bible verse to point to, but a growing knowledge of God's Word produces an internal sense of obligation to do what's right. That's why Psalm 119:9 says, "How can a young man keep his way pure? By living according to your word." It's important for children to know the Bible and understand biblical principles in order to increase conscience formation.

Children develop internal rules about how they will operate in life. Those internal rules are called *convictions*. Markus takes his shoes off at the door. That's just what they do in his family. It's developed into an internal rule, and because of that, he's now internally motivated to take his shoes off. If he were to wear his shoes in the house, he would feel uncomfortable, because the conscience would prompt him that it's just not right. But Markus feels very comfortable punching his younger brother and saying mean things to him. He needs some work to change what he believes and to develop an internal rule about how to treat his brother.

Using Rules to Teach Convictions

Family rules are one of the ways to teach convictions to children. After all, every rule in your family, whether written down or not, has a conviction behind it. Rules are based on convictions, and as children live in a family, they often learn convictions through those family rules. For example, Dad and Mom develop a rule in family life that says, "No punching other people and no put-downs." The rule is great, but it's made more valuable by sharing the convictions behind it. Dad and Mom consider their convictions and recognize that this is something they strongly believe because it comes out of their faith and their understanding of how God wants us to treat one another.

Dad and Mom call a family meeting and say to the boys, "We have a great family, and we enjoy our relationships quite a bit. In fact, we see you guys playing together, and it brings joy to our hearts. But we notice that sometimes you resort to punching and put-downs. We're going to work on this because we believe that it's not just a small problem. Your relationship together is valuable, and those little punches and comments can damage that relationship over time. It's a serious issue. Here's a Bible verse that will help us in this area. First Thessalonians 5:11 says, 'Encourage one another and build each other up.' That's a good verse for our family. We're going to work on that. If you punch or put down your brother, then you're going to have to do some building-up exercises. You'll need to think of three ways you can build up your brother, write them down, do them, and report to us." They prayed together as a family that God would give their boys the internal strength to do the right thing in their relationship.

Dad and Mom will be successful at helping Markus change. It will happen for a number of reasons. First, they're clarifying the conviction by articulating it as a rule in family life. Instead of simply taking away a privilege when the offense occurs, Dad and Mom are requiring that Markus practice doing the right thing. Over time, the tendencies will change and convictions will become strong enough to keep the desire to put others down in check.

Temptations occur in children just as they do in adults. When a child acts out and does the wrong thing, it's because emotions or desires become stronger than convictions and character. All these things are in the heart. Much of the work of parenting is identifying what heart quality needs development and then practicing it to increase internal strength.

> Much of the work of parenting is identifying what heart quality needs development and then practicing it to increase internal strength.

Talking about convictions and character helps kids see that there is a line between right and wrong. Although that line may be a bit different from one family to the next, the convictions you have in your family clarify that line for your children. You already have rules in family life. If you spend time talking about the convictions behind the rules, then you'll have opportunities to do conscience development. The values behind your family rules help children understand why your rules are different from other families', and even why the rules are important. The more you're able to strengthen the convictions of a child, the greater the internal motivation.

Convictions develop in children in ways other than talking about family rules. Sometimes it's a meaningful experience that helps a child develop a strong conviction about something. Abigail is eleven. When the neighbor next door was dying of lung cancer, her parents talked about the dangers of smoking. The neighbor continued to smoke even though the cigarettes were the cause of his impending death. That had a major effect on Abigail. She wasn't interested in even getting close to cigarettes. Based on an experience in her life, she developed a conviction and even a passion in her heart about smoking. Parents choose activities such as mission trips, books to read, and discussions to help guide the convictions their children develop.

Using God's Word to Form Convictions

God's Word is a powerful force for forming convictions. As children memorize and discuss Scripture, they develop a standard that feeds the conscience to make it strong and healthy. Kids often need help understanding God's Word and suggestions for making it practical. Spiritual formation for children is essential for their growth and has an amazing effect on internal motivation levels. Passing the faith on to your children does something deep within their hearts and helps them develop strong convictions about how they will live.

Keep in mind that telling kids what to do or simply teaching them information isn't enough to get it into their hearts. The heart contains a person's operating principles. You can often determine what those operating principles are by looking at your child's tendencies. A child who has a tendency to lie to get out of trouble has a conscience problem in the same way a child who can't accept responsibility for an offense or who is relentless in teasing does. Those behavioral tendencies reveal heart problems.

Much of the heart change takes place in a child through

prayer, study of God's Word, and by the grace of God at work in the child's life. However, the parent can do a lot to influence this heart change as well. One of the ways to change those tendencies is by repeating the right response over and over again.

Training the conscience involves teaching a child what the right thing is to do and then practicing it. If a child isn't doing well following instructions, part of the solution is to concentrate on that skill for a period of time. Some parents think they can just change the way they give an instruction and the child will change. Although that may happen sometimes, it usually takes some extra practice for a child to change the tendency to not follow instructions. It may take twenty practice instructions a day, in addition to the normal instructions, to heighten the learning curve for a child who needs to develop a new pattern.

As parents use a conscience approach to help children do what's right, they contribute to an internal sense of obligation in that child to do the right thing. The parents then are contributing to the child's sense of responsibility and maturity, and help build internal motivation.

5

When Kids Make Mistakes

The fear of making a mistake is like a prison.
Forgiveness is the key that unlocks the door.
Sometimes that forgiveness is toward self.

D ad and Mom were homeschooling their fourteen-year-old son, Gary, but were running into some signficant relational challenges in their home. Gary seemed to be hyper-sensitive to correction. Anytime Mom would correct him about his schoolwork—or anything else, for that matter—Gary would react poorly. He would defend himself and get angry. Their family needed help. Although they couldn't articulate it yet, they were running into challenges with their son in the area of the conscience that deals with wrongs.

The conscience prompts children with guilt when they've done the wrong thing. In fact, one of the functions of correction is to reveal a weakness, mistake, or sin. When children are faced with that reality, they often don't like it and don't know how to respond wisely. They may resort to all kinds of unhelpful and immature avoidance strategies. Some children have a tendency to blame, rationalize, or even get angry to protect themselves from their own guilt.

Guilt Can Be a Helpful Emotion

The challenge is to help children deal effectively with guilt in their lives. Guilt is a good emotion that points us toward repentance, and is not to be confused with shame. Guilt is a feeling of conviction for doing the wrong thing. Shame is a feeling of inadequacy because "I'm a failure." Guilt is a healthy emotion that motivates a person to admit an offense and take proper action to make amends. Shame is an unhealthy emotion that cripples a person with feelings of helplessness and hopelessness. Guilt can be used by God to prompt change. Shame is unhelpful and makes a person stop trying.

Parents can take advantage of the natural guilt that children feel as a result of the conscience and help them be internally motivated to deal properly with offenses. However, some parents make the mistake of using shame to get their kids' attention, drill the offense home, or somehow make an impression on the child. Sometimes parents even take out their own frustration on their kids by shaming them.

> Guilt is ultimately solved through the gift of Jesus Christ as the sacrifice for our sin.

Guilt is ultimately solved through the gift of Jesus Christ as the sacrifice for our sin. The most complete response to sin is to seek God's forgiveness through faith in Jesus. Then each person can do what's necessary to seek forgiveness from other people and make amends for an offense. Shame can prompt children to feel inadequate. One kid may have perfectionist tendencies that provide an internal message that says,

You'll never measure up. Another may have a fear that admitting an offense somehow makes him a bad person. These errors in thinking about guilt hinder a person's ability to respond properly to the conscience. You can help your child get rid of thinking errors and process offenses correctly.

Understanding the Value of Correction

One of the greatest gifts we can give our children is the ability to think rightly about their failures and process their weaknesses well. It starts by teaching children to value correction. That may seem impossible with some children, but it's an important place to start. You might share Proverbs 6:23, "The corrections of discipline are the way to life." The point is that correction is a good thing and can increase your quality of life.

Kids can learn things in a number of different ways. They can learn from a teacher, a parent, a coach, or from a video or a book, but one of the ways God has designed learning to take place is through correction. The problem is that some children believe that being corrected is a sign of weakness. It's not the fact that you're corrected that determines weakness. Rather, it's the response to correction that's important.

Gary's parents brought him to our office for counseling. I (Scott) met with the parents first and explained a bit about the conscience, about guilt, and how some kids are resistant to address offenses head-on and use manipulative techniques to try to avoid guilt. I explained that my goal would be to teach their son more about these same things and help him understand God's purpose for correction.

As I met with Gary, I asked him if I could share some scriptures with him. He was very open and realized that he had a problem with his anger. We talked about Proverbs 6:23 and the value of correction as a tool. Then I stopped and said, "You know, there's a verse in the Bible you're going to like. It's the stupid verse. Would you like to see that verse?"

Well, that surprised this young man. They didn't use the word "stupid" in their family. Frankly, I don't use that word in our family either, but the Bible uses the word. So I gave Gary a Bible and asked him to open it to Proverbs 12:1 and read it to me. He read it out loud: "'Whoever loves discipline loves knowledge, but he who hates correction is stupid.'" He started laughing. He couldn't believe the word *stupid* was in the Bible. I think he could hardly wait to tell others of his discovery.

> Correction is a good thing and can increase your quality of life.

I asked him, "Does it say there that the person who is corrected is stupid?"

"No," he replied. But most children believe that. They believe that if they're corrected it's because of some personal flaw in who they are as a person. If kids would only recognize that correction isn't a personal attack, and that, rather, it's a tool for growth, they would respond differently to the challenge.

I continued, "What does it say?"

"The person who hates correction is stupid."

"That's right. And how would a person demonstrate that he hates correction?"

"He might get angry."

"Yes, and what else?"

"He might have a bad attitude." At this point Gary began to see that he was describing himself.

We had a great conversation that day about the value of correction, and it had a marked impact on this young man. As Gary was leaving my office with his mom, he turned and said, "I'm not going to be stupid this week." His mom immediately got an odd expression on her face. I wonder what happened in their conversation on the way home. I was simply using God's Word to help Gary develop a new understanding of correction.

The problem isn't just a child's problem. If we're going to help our children learn to value correction, then it needs to start with the parents. Do you value correction? We're not just talking about you being corrected. We're also referring to the times you have to correct your children. The reality is that many parents feel irritated or annoyed with the correction process, in part, because they often feel that they're dealing with the same things over and over again every day. Or they're busy trying to get things done, and they're put out because they have to stop and correct a child.

Teaching Children the Value of Correction

Two things will help you handle correction times more effectively. One is margin in your day, and the other is a plan. Margin is that little extra time you build into your day to allow for unexpected correction. Remember that the most important conversation you have with a child in a day may happen during a correction time. If you're able to break through the defensiveness in a child, then you have a good opportunity to do significant heart work as your child wrestles with his or her mistakes or sin and determines to do better next time. It's all about teaching and training, and correction is an important part of that process.

Many children have a hard time with the value of correction, so we developed a game we play with kids in our office. We wanted to create a fun activity where children would have to fail in order to win the game. It goes this way: We randomly place twenty-eight hero cards upside down on the table; twenty-four of them have an exact match. The child turns one card over and then tries to remember where its match is. When he turns over a second card and it matches, he leaves them both faceup on the table. But when the cards don't match, he turns them back upside down and says the words, "Oops. I was wrong. I can learn from that." Many adults would benefit from playing this game because they sometimes play a different game and say to themselves, "Oops. I was wrong. I'm an idiot."

> Remember that the most important conversation you have with a child in a day may happen during a correction time.

The child has to say those words, "Oops. I was wrong. I can learn from that," over and over in the game. But that's not the only type of offense. Sometimes the wrong we do hurts others, and reconciliation is necessary. So, in the game, we put four "ouch" cards in the pile. Whenever an "ouch" card is revealed, the child then says, "Oops. I was wrong. Will you forgive me?" Many husbands and wives would benefit from playing this game to get in the habit of asking forgiveness, instead of the popular marriage game that says, "Oops. I was wrong. It's your fault."

As children say those two phrases over and over again, they're building a pattern in the game. Then it's easier for them to make those statements in real life. The point we're trying to teach children is that correction is a valuable tool in their lives, and it's a way to learn and grow. God wants us to learn from mistakes, not beat ourselves up or attack other people.

Ending Discipline Times Well

The second important component to handling correction well is a good plan. Those parents who don't have a good plan often resort to reactive parenting, simply seeing problems and reacting in ways that may not always be best. Thinking through how to respond to particular challenges ahead of time can equip you to handle the daily correction needs in your family. Think in advance of how you want to respond when your children are fighting, whining, or showing disrespect. Develop a plan and you'll likely have more control of yourself instead of reacting in surprise.

One way to strengthen a child's conscience is to end discipline times with a *positive conclusion* because it teaches children a specific plan for dealing with the uncomfortable feeling they have when they've made a mistake or have deliberately done the wrong thing. Every time you correct or redirect your kids, we would recommend you process the offense with them using this approach. Although it may appear to be a formula, children learn through routine, and this approach can teach them a way to think when they've made a mistake or done something wrong.

The positive conclusion consists of three questions and a statement. We developed the positive conclusion as we studied the biblical concept of repentance and the thinking process people must go through to repent. The Greek word for *repentance* used in the Bible means "a change of mind." As parents correct their children, that's what they're looking for. It's more than just behavior change; it's a heart change that's important. As children go through the positive conclusion over and over again, they're learning not just how to deal with the current offense but how to think about offenses in general.

The First Question: Confession

Question #1 starts the process with confession: "What did you do wrong?" If someone is going to change, then confession of a weakness or an offense is a good start. By answering this question, children learn to take responsibility for their part of the problem. Sometimes parents ask different questions, such as,

"Who started it?" When you ask that question, you teach your children to be defensive, because kids can typically think of all the offenses of others before they think of their own. Rarely when asked the question, "Who started it?" does a child say, "I did." Unfortunately, many parents actually train their children to be defensive by asking the wrong questions.

Even if the child didn't start it, and is only 10 percent of the problem, that child still needs to take responsibility for that 10 percent. Kids need to learn how to respond well when others are doing the wrong thing or offend them. It's all part of dealing with conflict. In one family, James, age twelve, continually blamed problems on others. Mom began using a different approach. She asked, "What percent of the problem was yours?"

Her son would typically respond, "It was only 10 percent my problem."

"Okay," said Mom. "Let's talk about your 10 percent. What did you do wrong?"

Some children, when asked, "What did you do wrong?" respond with, "I don't know" or "I didn't do anything wrong." And sometimes they genuinely don't know. You have your son take a break for a bit, and he sits there for a half hour and totally forgets what he did wrong. In that case, you might tell him what he did wrong, but don't just tell him and have him agree. Repeat the question and have him confess. Confession is an important spiritual skill, and practicing it as you end correction times is a great way to help children learn and grow.

Of course, some children respond with "I don't know" when you know they do know what they did wrong. If your child does this, you might have him go take a break again and tell him, "When you remember, come back and see me." It's amazing how quickly some children remember when there are no other alternatives.

Sometimes children must wrestle in their hearts for a bit in

WHEN KIDS MAKE MISTAKES

order to come to a place of humility and admit what they did wrong. Having a child take a break for an undefined time period can help him work through the issue of guilt in a healthier way. Some parents make the mistake of sending a child to a time-out for a certain number of minutes, usually corresponding to the child's age. Rarely does that length of time correspond to the child's need to process the offense. Sending a child on a mission to change the heart and return when ready may take a half hour or even an hour sometimes. The point is that the child must first settle down and then wrestle with the issue until he or she is ready to confess. That process can take a bit of time but is very productive, as it forces the child to do some internal processing of the offense.

The idea of wrestling in one's heart is seen in God's Word on a number of occasions. In Matthew 9:4, Jesus, knowing that the teachers

> Question #1 starts the process with confession: "What did you do wrong?"

of the law were struggling in their hearts, said to them, "Why do you entertain evil thoughts in your hearts?" Mary, the mother of Jesus, was amazed by the shepherds' excitement over the infant Jesus, and Luke 2:19 says that she pondered all these things in her heart. Although Mary wasn't necessarily wrestling with the things she was experiencing, notice that the pondering took place in the heart. Similarly, correction becomes one of those tools that helps children do some necessary internal pondering or wrestling, coming to a place where they're ready to admit a weakness or confess a mistake. The first question in the positive conclusion is strategic for heart change.

The Second Question: Getting to the Heart

"What did you do wrong?" tends to focus on behavior. The second question, "Why was that wrong?" gets down to the heart.

As you're working with older children, even teenagers, this is a great teaching question that helps determine underlying values, convictions, and motivations. This question often leads to valuable discussions with children about the deeper ramifications of their actions.

Every child is, or should be, working on some kind of heart quality. If your fifteen-year-old is doing poorly at school because he forgets to turn in his homework, he's doing more than just changing his behavior. He's working on thoroughness or diligence. If your nine-year-old often says hurtful things to her brother, she needs to work on changing her heart and becoming more kind. Your three-year-old may need to work on patience and waiting with a happy heart. One of the tools you'll use to develop character in your child is correction. If you view correction as an interruption to your day, then you may react poorly and miss good opportunities for growth. The second question, "Why was that wrong?" helps kids see that their particular offense ties into something much bigger that exists in the heart.

You can use the positive conclusion with younger children, but they will likely have a hard time answering this question, so you may want to make it multiple choice. If you have three basic rules in your family, such as obey, show honor, and be kind, then most any offense a preschooler can commit falls under one of those values. Then, when you ask the question, "Why was that wrong?" a preschooler can choose from one of those three rules. Now the positive conclusion contributes to the teaching of those family rules through practical dialogue and mistakes a child has made.

The Third Question: Developing a Plan for Next Time

The third question—"What are you going to do differently next time?"—turns the conversation to the future. It gets kids thinking about the "next times" of life. And not just the kids. It's also important to get parents thinking about a plan for next time. Essentially, through this question, you're helping your child develop a strategy to overcome the temptation by having a plan for next time. "How are you going to respond better next time when I tell you that you can't have a snack right now?" Or, "What are you going to say and do when your brother takes your iPod without asking?"

> The third question—"What are you going to do differently next time?"—turns the conversation to the future.

Repentance isn't just stopping something. It's a 180-degree turn, choosing to do something *right* instead. So when parents work with their children to plan the next times of life, they're helping build confidence, hope, and proper thinking. Too many times in the correction experience, parents focus on what the child did wrong. The third question of the positive conclusion helps children focus on what they can do right the next time.

It's not one positive conclusion that will change a child's heart. Change takes time. Many children know in their heads what they need to do. If you ask your son, he'll likely tell you that he should be kind to his sister. He knows it in his head, but when she takes his iPod without asking, the operating principles in his heart say, "Revenge." By going through a positive conclusion over and over again, the training helps children move the ideas from the head to the heart. Furthermore, you're educating the conscience and teaching your child how to respond to the uncomfortable feeling of guilt that the conscience provides. Only the most mature children—and adults, for that matter—learn how to think rightly about offenses. This training is a primary work of conscience formation in a child's life.

Many children know the right thing to do, but they don't know how to apply it in a given situation. When you answer the third question, you'll want to be specific so your child understands how to do what's right next time.

Answers to question #3 help a child learn how to respond to interruptions with a good attitude, or what to do and say when her brother is annoying. This may be a brainstorming session, but it results in a plan for the child for the next time.

Ending Discipline Times with Hope

After the three questions, it's important to make the final statement, "Okay. Go ahead and try again." This is a statement of affirmation that basically says, "I believe in you. We've talked about this and identified a better response for next time. Go ahead and try it out." Children need this final statement because it helps provide hope as they continue to face the challenges of life. It's like what Jesus said to the woman caught in adultery in John 8:11: "Go, and sin no more" (KJV).

That verse is a conscience-freeing message that children need to learn to say to themselves. Some kids beat themselves up over and over again because of mistakes they make. Other children feel inadequate or consider themselves failures. They all need that final statement. A parent's affirmation goes a long way to help children move past mistakes. The positive conclusion is a gift you give to your children to teach them how to think rightly about their offenses.

We developed this last statement in the positive conclusion after looking at ways that God and Jesus disciplined people in the Bible. They often had a forward-looking meeting during a correction time. For example, the consequence in Genesis 3 was that Adam and Eve were banished from the garden of Eden and could never come back. But God didn't just give the consequence and go on from there. He had a meeting with them, and he looked at the clothes they were wearing. He saw that the fig leaves they had sewn together were inadequate for them, probably because they reminded Adam and Eve of the garden and their past sin. So God made new clothes for them out of animal skins. And he gave them a promise that someday the seed from the woman would crush the serpent's head. God gave them hope. He ended the discipline time with a positive conclusion, a good model for us as parents.

When Jesus appeared to Peter after the resurrection, he asked him three times, "Peter, do you love me?" Why three times? Maybe because just a few days earlier, Peter had denied Christ three times. He had lied about not even knowing the Savior.

Peter answered the question three times in John 21:15–17, "Yes, I love you." And notice Jesus' response. He focused on the future, not the past. He said, "Feed my lambs," "Take care of my sheep," and "Feed my sheep." In essence, Jesus was saying to Peter, "Come on, Peter; let's move forward. We have a kingdom to build." And just a few days later, God chose one man to stand up on the day of Pentecost and preach a sermon to which three thousand people responded. Whom did he choose? The man who had lied three times. Jesus restored Peter and used him mightily in his kingdom program.

That's the same message you want your children to hear. They sin and make mistakes, but God can still use them. The key is threefold: repentance, confession, and forgiveness.

Let's look at one more beautiful story. After David sinned with Bathsheba, the prophet Nathan came in and told the story of the man who stole another man's lamb, appealing to David's conscience. David was incensed by the injustice. He demanded that the perpetrator be held to account for his misdeeds. Nathan then revealed that David was the man. At that point David knew his sin was exposed. The consequence was that his baby died. It took seven days for that child to die, probably because God needed that period of time to work in David's heart. But the Bible tells us in 2 Samuel 12:24–25, "Then David comforted his wife Bathsheba, and he went to her and made love to her. She gave birth to a son, and they named him Solomon. The LORD loved him; and because the LORD loved him, he sent word through Nathan the prophet to name him Jedidiah." That name means "loved by the Lord." What was God doing? He was having a positive conclusion with David and Bathsheba. In essence, he was saying to them, "Come on; the sin is done. Your consequence is over. We have a kingdom to build. Let's go forward here."

Those words, I'm sure, were a gift that David and Bathsheba needed in their hearts. It was a conscience-freeing statement that helped them experience God's forgiveness in a tangible way. God is in the business of cleansing the conscience.

In fact, as parents work toward a positive conclusion with their children, they're demonstrating the way God relates to us. First John 1:9 makes it clear: "If we confess our sins, he is faithful and just and will forgive us our sins and purify us from all unrighteousness." God wants to purify the conscience, to cleanse it from guilt. That happens first as we accept Christ as Savior and Lord, and then as we confess our sins to him and seek his grace every day.

Children need to know how to process offenses, how to respond to guilt, and how to receive forgiveness. Many of the day-to-day correction times you have with your children are opportunities to reflect who God is and how he handles sin. As you do the work of discipline day after day, you have the ability to strengthen the conscience by your approach and by the conversations you have.

Asking the three questions and making that statement are not just childish tools that children will outgrow. They are a mature response to offenses, mistakes, sins, and weaknesses that children will use for the rest of their lives. One of the primary reasons children lack internal motivation to deal with wrongs is because of misbeliefs and the inability to process mistakes and sins properly. By working on the positive conclusion and teaching kids to value correction, you are often opening new doors for kids that allow them to process offenses on their own. They are becoming internally motivated and even empowered to address the guilt that the conscience provides. After all, many adults have a poor response to correction. They end up blaming or justifying their faults instead of taking responsibility for them. The positive conclusion is an adult skill. Kids who learn the process in childhood develop a powerful tool they'll use for the rest of their lives.

The positive conclusion is only one piece of a good correction routine, but it's an important step in the process. Children may still need a consequence or may have to make restitution, apologize, or reconcile with someone, but the positive conclusion prepares them with a way to think, helping address the conscience in one of its most sensitive areas.

One of the goals that parents have, or should have, is to equip their kids to handle offenses well. Most children have a problem in this area and need a bit of work to become more comfortable addressing their own mistakes and weaknesses. Part of internal motivation training encourages children to take initiative, but because we are imperfect people, that initiative sometimes results in mistakes, sins, or offenses. Training children to value correction and to respond well to wrongs in their lives prepares them for life. Teaching children about the conscience and its prompting to address errors, both unintentional and deliberate, is a great tool for life.

6

Learning to Value Integrity

Honesty is the first chapter in the book of relationship success.

Honesty is a conscience issue. In fact, good moral development is often revealed in a person's ability to demonstrate honesty in difficult situations. With training, kids can develop an internal motivation to keep their integrity instead of sacrificing it for some temporary benefit. Consider these three stories of young people who were dishonest and were brought to our office for help.

> Good moral development is often revealed in a person's ability to demonstrate honesty in difficult situations.

Brian, age seventeen, stole his father's credit card and bought jewelry for his girlfriend. I (Scott) was so intrigued by the story that, in private, I asked him what he was thinking. "Did you think that you wouldn't get caught?"

"Oh, I knew I'd get caught, but I just figured it would blow over."

Brian didn't realize what he'd lost.

Marcy, age sixteen, was caught drinking by the police after sneaking out of the house. We worked together for several months over one summer. During much of that time, she was grounded, unable to spend time with her friends. At the end of the summer, I said to her, "Now you're going back to school. You'll be with friends again. How are you going to prevent this problem from happening another time?"

"I won't do that again," she said. "I've developed a relationship with my dad these past months that I don't want to lose." Her internal motivation to be open and honest instead of deceptive took a huge leap that summer.

On that same day, a third young person was in my office because her parents looked at her text messages and realized that she was engaged in something that was against family values. She had been dishonest with her parents, and now they had a problem.

> If your child is young, or doesn't have a problem in the area of integrity, don't assume you don't need to worry about it.

In each of these cases, the young person had lost something very valuable: they lost their integrity. They each needed to learn more about what it actually was that they lost. We taught them about the *integrity package* and what it contained. All three then realized the ramifications of what they had done and were motivated to regain their integrity. We helped them do it.

If your child is young, or doesn't have a problem in this area, don't assume you don't need to worry about it. Teaching about the benefits of a life of integrity is essential to safeguard children for the future. Kids need self-motivation to be honest and are faced with temptations regularly to cut corners and sacrifice their integrity for things they want. Parents never know when a child will become tempted to be dishonest. Your work to build a strong conscience in the area of honesty will benefit your child well into adulthood.

The Integrity Package

The *integrity package* contains several benefits. A discussion about what it is and why it's valuable can help increase a child's internal motivation in day-to-day opportunities to demonstrate honesty. If you're honest, you get these benefits. If you're dishonest, you lose them. It's helpful for children to understand the integrity package before they do damage to relationships with dishonesty, but it's certainly helpful when they want to build the road back. The integrity package contains the following four things.

The *benefit of the doubt* is one of the privileges in the integrity package. It's the tendency to believe someone when there's some question about the truth. We tend to give people the benefit of the doubt, whether we know them or not. If a complete stranger comes up and tells you something, you tend to believe it. That's the benefit of the doubt.

If Dad comes into the kitchen and puts five dollars down on the counter, and then comes back fifteen minutes later and it's gone, he has a problem. If his eleven-year-old daughter, Jill, has never stolen any money, then he doesn't consider her having taken it. He gives Jill the benefit of the doubt. However, if Jill has taken money in the past, doubt arises in his mind: *I wonder if Jill took it?* Later, he may find out that his wife picked it up, and Jill wasn't guilty at all. The point is that when someone is dishonest, he or she loses the benefit of the doubt.

A second component of the integrity package is *trustworthiness*. The person who is trustworthy receives extra privileges and opportunities. For example, if Jude is trustworthy, then Mom says, "I'm going over to the neighbor's for a couple of minutes. You stay here and work on your homework." If Jude is not trustworthy, she says, "I'm going over to the neighbor's for a couple of minutes. Come on; you're going with me."

Trustworthiness allows a person more freedom, extra autonomy, and a bit more independence. You don't want to lose the integrity package. It contains some valuable things.

A third benefit of the integrity package is the *privilege of privacy*. Parents have the responsibility of checking up on their kids, but when children are honest, parents can give their children more privacy. When a child has a habit of dishonesty, parents do more checking of their text messages, monitoring their computer history, and looking around in the bedroom. Privacy is a privilege one doesn't want to lose.

> Trustworthiness allows a person more freedom, extra autonomy, and a bit more independence.

A fourth benefit of the integrity package is the *internal peace* you have when you do the right thing. If you're called to the principal's office and you've been dishonest, you immediately think, *Uh-oh. They found out.* But if you're in the habit of doing what's right, you say, "That's interesting. I wonder what he wants." If you've been dishonest and your mom calls your name from the other room, you immediately panic and wonder if you've been caught. If you've been doing what's right, you don't have that dreadful feeling. There's something quite freeing inside when you're in the habit of doing what's right. That peace is something happening inside the conscience of a child. In fact, that desire for peace is what builds internal motivation to be honest on a daily basis.

Building the Road Back

If you do a study of dishonesty in the Bible, one character seems to stand above all others when it comes to lying and sneakiness. His name was Jacob, and even his name means "deceitful one." He was the one who stole the birthright from his brother and tricked his father out of the blessing that was supposed to go to his brother. Jacob had to run for his life and go live with, and work for, his uncle Laban. He never saw his mother again.

At some point in his life, Jacob became tired of his dishonest ways. He decided that he would make a change. It's not exactly clear when that happened. Maybe it took place when he wrestled with the angel, and God changed his name from Jacob, or "deceiver," to Israel, which means "God prevails." But maybe the change started happening much earlier. Laban had given Jacob all his speckled or spotted sheep and goats, and all the dark-colored lambs, as his wages. Now take a look at Genesis 30:33 and read Jacob's words to his boss: "My honesty will testify for me in the future, whenever you check on the wages you have paid me. Any goat in my possession that is not speckled or spotted, or any lamb that is not dark-colored, will be considered stolen." Not only was Jacob trying to prove his honesty, but he was also teaching us the solution for children who want to build the road back and regain the integrity package.

In fact, it's these words that helped all three young people discussed at the beginning of this chapter regain their integrity. They all began building the road back. First, let's look at the verse; then we'll show you how integrity is rebuilt.

"My honesty will testify for me in the future, whenever you check on the wages you have paid me. Any goat in my possession that is not speckled or spotted, or any lamb that is not dark-colored, will be considered stolen." The key words are "check on."

When a parent checks on a child and finds the child has done the right thing, the process of rebuilding trust begins.

Parents want to trust their children, but trust doesn't just happen because they're your kids. Trust happens when children are reliable, do what they say they are going to do, and are honest. When young people have been dishonest, they lose the trust of others, but they can earn it back. When they determine to allow God to do a deeper work in their lives and commit to being honest, they have nothing to hide. They can invite their parents to check up on them. The attitude of the parent when checking up on kids is important. Mom or Dad isn't seeking to find out if a child has done the wrong thing, but instead the parent is looking to find the child trustworthy. The parent and child work together to rebuild trust. Parents want to trust their children. But trust comes with small steps of trustworthiness over time.

> Parents want to trust their children, but trust doesn't just happen because they're your kids.

Imagine the road back built by many bricks. A child stands at one end of the road and, by being honest and inviting a parent to check up on him, is trying to rebuild trust and regain the integrity package. Each time Dad or Mom checks up on him, it's like picking up a brick and seeing if it is sturdy underneath and then placing it down again. It's not just one brick that rebuilds integrity. In fact, I tell kids that it often takes about five hundred bricks to rebuild trust. You need to get into the habit of being checked up on. Furthermore, if there's some bad news, make sure you're the one to report it to your parents instead of having them find out from the teacher, coach, or a friend's parents. That goes a long way to setting bricks down on your road of trust.

Keeping Developmental Stages in Mind

Keep in mind a child's developmental stage as you process this idea of dishonesty. For example, preschoolers often engage in what's called "magical thinking." Because their imagination is developing at that age, they often get confused with what's true and what's not. Many preschool books have stories about animals that talk, so a preschooler might tell you a story about a squirrel that passed on a message. In those cases, it's important to do some teaching. "Since squirrels don't really talk, it would be better for you to say, 'Wouldn't it be fun if the squirrel gave me a message?' or 'I wish a squirrel would tell *me* something.'" Preschoolers often need help communicating fantasy so it doesn't appear to be dishonest.

Children at any age struggle with how to use the truth in socially challenging situations. For example, a six-year-old might point to a person standing outside a store and say to her mom, "That person is smoking. He's going to get cancer." Although it may be true and reflective of things taught at home, it's not appropriate to always share everything you know. You don't have to be dishonest, but wisdom often requires discernment about when and how to use the truth.

When a twelve-year-old leaves a boring party and is asked by the host, "Did you have fun?" how should she respond? Should she lie in order not to hurt the person's feelings? Even if the answer is no, that doesn't mean she tells the person that it's the most boring party she's ever been to. Kids need to understand what tact is and how to respond graciously and honestly in tough situations.

Some children use teasing as an excuse for lying. When caught in a lie and to excuse themselves, they say, "I was just teasing."

That's wrong, of course, but kids don't always understand the line between something that is dishonest and something that is just untrue. Take this example.

Tobias comes into the kitchen and asks Mom, "What's for dinner?"

Mom replies, "Frog soup." Is Mom lying? No, she's teasing by saying something that's not true. Those who define lying as saying something that isn't true miss the mark. Sometimes a person says something that's not true and is just wrong or mistaken. That isn't necessarily lying.

Lying is using words or symbols with the intent to deceive. Both Tobias and Mom know they aren't having frog soup. Mom is joking with her son. However, if Tobias thinks he can cover up a lie by saying it was teasing, he's missing the point. What's the difference? Tobias was trying to deceive. Of course, sometimes the line between the two can get quite fuzzy. Because of that, some parents take a break from teasing or stop altogether in order to help their children develop a clear sense of honesty. Teasing isn't wrong. It's often a fun way to interact together in family life and contributes to connected relationships. But teasing always has a line, and when that line is crossed, problems happen. We must guard the line and teach children to recognize when they've crossed it.

If you have a child who struggles with honesty, you'll want to do several things to help build internal motivation to uphold integrity. It's helpful to have regular discussions about the truth and about having the internal courage to speak the truth even when it's hard. Life often provides temptations to lie, cheat, or steal to avoid getting into trouble or to obtain something a child wouldn't be able to get otherwise. Some children lie because they have a poor view of themselves or because they, themselves, don't trust others. It takes internal strength to do what's right in those situations. Being dishonest is a sign of weakness, not a sign of strength, contrary to what children sometimes believe. Many children take shortcuts in life, and dishonesty is only a symptom of an inability to work hard. Many parents can help their kids by giving them more chores and difficult tasks to build the heart qualities of determination and perseverance.

It's often helpful to pray and ask God to reveal times when your child is doing the wrong thing or trying to get away with something without getting caught. God often reveals to parents information that helps them take action and expose the dishonesty. These

Some children use teasing as an excuse for lying.

events provide an opportunity to teach that dishonesty isn't worth it. Furthermore, parents whose children easily give in to the temptation to be dishonest need to be more vigilant, and they should check up on their children. This vigilance often strengthens the conscience. It creates a discomfort for the child that often translates into an internal dialogue. The child says, "I better not do this, or I might get caught." Although this isn't the best form of internal motivation, it does help children see that lying and dishonesty aren't worth it. The goal is that, over time, children will recognize the danger of habits of dishonesty and then look for ways to build integrity in their lives.

Children who lie often think they won't get caught, no one is watching, or their offense will somehow be overlooked. One of the important realities of life is that God is always watching. We don't want our children to view God as a cosmic policeman, but instead to recognize that God sees the difficult situations we find ourselves in, understands our desires, and offers us strength and power to do what's right, even when it's hard. God promises us grace, and when kids gain a larger understanding of what grace is, it helps them live their everyday lives.

Grace doesn't look the other way when someone sins. But grace does identify with our weaknesses, giving us the strength to handle the tough times and empowering us to trust God for his answers in his time.

Integrity is one of those qualities that defines a person's sensitivity to faith and morality. Emphasizing it in family life is strategic. It may take years to help a child overcome a habit of lying, but your hard work over time pays off to communicate the importance of living a life of integrity and thus strengthens a child's conscience.

7

Compassion: Thinking Beyond Oneself

If you want your kids to fly straight,
teach them obedience. If you want
them to fly high, teach them honor.

"Teresa is self-centered. She is ten years old and thinks the whole world revolves around her." Charity continued to describe her three kids. "Ronald is fourteen, and he gets so irritated with her and his little brother that he's always putting them both down and making sarcastic remarks. I don't know what to do. Our home is a miserable place."

As we listened to Charity share her story, we felt her pain. Mom knew that if something didn't change, the patterns she saw in her kids would damage their relationships both now and in the future. We were eager to help this mom because we've seen families like this change over time to remove toxic patterns and embrace nurturing ones. We started by helping Mom think of each child individually and then develop a plan of action. Since Teresa tended to be self-centered, we knew that a conscience approach focusing on caring about others was a great place to start.

It's always encouraging to see a child who naturally thinks about others. This child may see that you're sad and come over to give a hug, want to help people in a third world country have food to eat, or see a hurt bird and want to provide care. That sensitivity is a gift and demonstrates internal motivation, prompted by the conscience.

Most children, however, need work in this area, and parents can do a lot to help. Since kids can have a tendency to think mainly about themselves, what they want, what they need, or how they can be happy, some training is required to develop the new way of thinking. Part of that training will focus on what children believe, and another part will concentrate on practical ways to change how they act.

Helping Kids Develop Compassion

To motivate children to develop new patterns, parents often have to stretch their kids beyond the tendency to be selfish by requiring that they look for ways to think of others. A great place to start is with God's Word. God designed our world and knows what works most effectively. He has given us principles that will guide our thinking.

For example, Philippians 2:3–4 says, "Do nothing out of selfish ambition or vain conceit, but in humility consider others better than yourselves. Each of you should look not only to your own interests, but also to the interests of others." That's a great family verse and can help get kids thinking of ways to contribute to the well-being of others.

Romans 12:10 is our favorite verse for this area of the conscience: "Honor one another above yourselves." That verse is for all people, not just children. However, honor is one of the quali-ties learned at home. Eight times in the Bible it says, "Honor your father and mother." In fact, according to Ephesians 6:1–3, there are two parts to a child's job description: obedience and honor. God has created a conscience inside a child that can be trained with those two principles. As children learn obedience, they're learning to do what's right. As children learn honor, they're learning to think about others.

"Honor one another above yourselves." That verse is for all people, not just children.

Hebrews 13:18 ties the concept of living honorably with the con-science: "We are sure that we have a clear conscience and desire to live honorably in every way." The conscience God places inside a person provides an internal satisfaction when that individual does something kind for others.

You feel good when you allow someone else to go first or have the best seat. In that moment you often feel a sense of great-ness, having risen above the crowd.

That's what Jesus was trying to teach his disciples when he said to them in Mark 10:42–44, "You know that those who are regarded as rulers of the Gentiles lord it over them, and their high officials exercise authority over them. Not so with you. Instead, whoever wants to become great among you must be your servant, and whoever wants to be first must be slave of all." In fact, when we consider others or serve others, we become like Jesus. That's why he added in verse 45, "For even the Son of Man did not come to be served, but to serve, and to give his life as a ransom for many."

Teresa needed to think about others, become more aware of how her actions were affecting others, and then make some significant changes in how she lived and operated. We helped

Charity use the biblical concept of honor to increase sensitivity in her daughter.

Honor is a practical tool for conscience development, and teaching about honor can raise a child's internal motivation in the area of thinking about others. We define *honor* in simple terms for children. As we see the concept taught in God's Word, we say that honor is treating people as special, doing more than what's expected, and having a good attitude. That's a working definition of honor, helping children know how to put honor into practice. Even young children can memorize that definition. But honor isn't just for young children. We tell teens that God has hidden within honor the secret ingredients you'll need to be successful in life. When you treat others as special, it often comes back to you. Let's take that honor definition, look at its three parts, and discuss how to use it in family life.

First of all, the essence of honor is treating people as special. The Greek word used in the New Testament for honor is *timae* and means "value." In the Old Testament the word is *cavod* and means "heavy." The idea of both is that we treat others as valuable. Some parents think that teaching honor simply means training their children to have good manners. But honor is more than that. Manners focus on behavior. Honor comes from the heart. It's a very practical concept for family life, but most children need a bit of help to understand and develop it. Obedience gets the job done, but honor deals with how that job is done. Honor is a relational term. Bad attitudes, whining, and complaining are honor issues. Honor helps develop compassion because it helps children to be internally motivated to think outside themselves and contribute to *others'* lives.

> Obedience gets the job done, but honor deals with how that job is done.

Of course, the enemy of honor is selfishness, a me-first atti-tude that hinders a person from treating others as special. If you're seeing any kind of selfishness in your child, then remember that for every form of selfishness, there's an honor-based solution. Many kids, and adults, too, are internally motivated to think about self. Honor raises the bar and provides the conscience with practical tools for moving beyond self and thinking of others.

Illustrating Honor as a Gift

Honor is like giving a gift. Kids like to give gifts. They enjoy planning surprises for people. That's a way of treating people as special. Take advantage of this desire and plan a gift or a sur-prise for someone. Then call it honor. Kids will soon catch the relationship between the two and recognize that honor can be used in many ways in relationships to do extra, provide a special surprise, and enhance the atmosphere.

You, as a parent, are likely honoring your children already in a number of ways. When you go to the store, you bring home your son's favorite cookies. Why? Because you like to see the delight on his face. You might say, "Son, I wanted to honor you by getting your favorite cookies." It won't be long before you're asking him to demonstrate honor in your family as well.

But how do you get kids to show honor? It's hard to teach someone to give you a gift. One mom taught honor this way. She told her son that he needed to set the table for dinner. That's obe-dience. But then when he was done, he needed to add one more thing. That's honor. If he needed ideas, she could offer them, but he needed to choose for himself. He might make a center-piece, create name cards or place mats, or put ice in the glasses. "Make your choice and do it; then come back and show me what you did." Her son chose to make a little paper airplane for each person at the table. When the family came to dinner and saw the planes, smiles were shared. Mom said, "Our dinner tastes even better when honor is at the table."

If two children tend to fight, bicker, and compete with each other, it may be time to initiate honor therapy. When you see some form of dishonor or meanness, you might require that your son think of two honor things he can do for his brother before he's free to go. It takes work to change bad habits and patterns of meanness, but practicing honor several times a day can be just the strategy needed to turn bad habits into good ones.

> If two children tend to fight, bicker, and compete with each other, it may be time to initiate honor therapy.

Honor builds the conscience because it increases the internal sense of obligation to treat others kindly. As parents reinforce the idea that honor is not optional and that everyone has a responsibility to treat others well, kids begin to feel uncomfortable with mistreatment.

We helped Charity develop a plan for Ronald too. He also needed honor, but the techniques and strategies for him were a bit different. Ronald had a problem. He was continually irritated by his younger siblings, and he didn't know how to handle his frustration. When irritated, he was tempted to use put-downs and sarcasm to communicate his displeasure. That needed to change.

Ronald knew that his mistreatment of his siblings was wrong. He needed a better plan, and he needed to change the habits of meanness he had developed. Mom gave Ronald a vision for changing himself, even if his siblings didn't change. He could become a more nurturing person. Their ability to change wasn't as important as Ronald's ability to respond well in a difficult situation. Charity also used firmness and practice as she coached Ronald to contribute significantly to family life. In fact, Ronald learned more than to treat his sister and brother more kindly. He also began implementing another part of the honor definition, doing more than what's expected.

Teaching Kids to Do More Than What's Expected

The second part of the honor definition is doing more than what's expected. It comes from such Bible directives as, "Turn the other cheek" (Matthew 5:39); "Go the extra mile" (Matthew 5:41); "Love your enemies" (Matthew 5:44); "Bless those who persecute you" (Romans 12:14); "If your enemy is hungry, feed him" (Romans 12:20); and others that demonstrate the same idea. Each of those commands indicates a way of living that does more than what's expected.

To practice this at home, you might encourage children to do extra things to surprise people. One dad told this story: "I wanted to teach my sons how to honor their mother, so while she was out, we decided to prepare for her arrival home. I asked the boys to help think of suggestions. They had to demonstrate compassion by thinking about Mom's needs and what she liked. We came up with a number of ideas so that when Mom came in the door, we greeted her with a hug, brought her a drink, and took her packages out of her hands so she could sit down and rest while the boys and I finished making dinner. Mom felt honored, and everyone enjoyed the process."

This part of the honor definition teaches children initiative. They learn to be internally motivated to look for things that need to be done and to do something about them. The child who learns honor does better at school, for example, because she is continually looking for one extra thing to do to make the assignment better or to help out in the classroom.

Charity partnered with Ronald to look for ways to add energy to their family. Ronald would look for ways to contribute to family life. Sometimes he would need some prompting, but Mom was encouraged by the positive change she was seeing in her son. He was getting it, and family life was taking on a better tone.

If you're going to teach honor, you'll have to allow your child to choose what to do. That makes teaching honor a bit tricky. Look for ways to teach honor as part of following instructions, but be careful that you allow the child some initiative in the process. If you tell him to clean up the bathroom, that's obedience. But if you tell him to go into the bathroom and "take an honor look," and he sees what needs to be done and does it, that's honor. The key is that the child has to think of what to do. To show honor in this way, the child must consider the other person's needs and feelings. That's where the conscience gets its exercise. When kids have to figure out what is right or do something to care for someone else without being told, you're developing initiative and internal motivation.

Good Attitudes Are
Essential, Not Optional

The third part of the honor definition encourages children to have a good attitude. Some children act under the misconception that if they're disappointed or unhappy, they have the right to display their displeasure and make everyone else miserable. Philippians 2:5 says, "Your attitude should be the same as that of Christ Jesus." Verse 14 of that chapter says, "Do everything without complaining or arguing." The idea is that your attitude is a sign of your obedience to God.

Some parents excuse a child's attitude by saying things like, "He's a boy," or "She's a teenager," or "She's had a hard day," or "He's tired." When we rationalize a child's bad attitude, we miss an opportunity to teach honor. An attitude affects the climate in a room. In the same way that putting trash in a lake pollutes the water, a bad attitude puts a damper on the emotional environment in a home. As you help your children consider others, even when they feel upset, you're teaching them about an internal obligation. You're strengthening the conscience.

Charity illustrated this idea to her kids. She took a plastic bucket and put holes in the bottom so water could drip out. They hung the bucket from a tree low enough for the children to be able to reach it. About twenty feet away was a large bucket full of water. The goal was for Mom and the kids to work together to fill the bucket with water. Of course, the bucket leaked, so it required that they work extra hard to keep it filled. Afterward they sat down on the grass, read the above verses from Philippians, and had a discussion. As the bucket continued to leak, everyone kept looking over to the bucket. It was a great illustration.

> Philippians 2:5 says, "Your attitude should be the same as that of Christ Jesus."

Charity said, "If we imagine that the bucket is our family, and the water is the energy we need to keep our family doing well, then whose job is it to fill the bucket? What if only Mom filled the bucket? Would it remain full of water? Probably not. When everyone in the family is working together to add energy to family life, we all enjoy the benefits. If someone has a bad attitude, argues, or whines, it's like adding another hole to the bucket."

They continued to talk about ways to add energy to family life and how people sometimes hinder that energy. They then prayed together that God would strengthen their family and that each person might be helpful in that process. Over the next few days there were several opportunities to refer back to the bucket.

It's interesting to see what happens to children who catch a vision for honor. For some kids it takes a lot of work, but over time, kids begin to feel uncomfortable with selfishness and feel an inner obligation to consider others. Sometimes the feeling of compassion isn't there, but a child makes a decision to do the right thing and share a treat, or allows someone to have a turn in the game. It's over time that compassion develops.

It took a lot of work, but Charity saw significant changes in her family. The kids were handling conflict, annoyance, and challenges better, and the framework of honor was changing them in positive ways. Mom continued to work with each of her kids individually to strengthen the conscience in the area of caring about others. They even planned ways that they could show honor together to those outside the family. Charity began to regularly ask at dinner, "What random act of kindness did you do today?" It was fun to hear the children report. Mom has created a culture in their family in which showing honor is expected every day. It takes a lot of work to help children move from selfishness to an others-centered way of living. But helping children in this area strengthens the conscience and builds in them the internal obligation to carry it out with friends, and with others as well.

Much of the work of conscience development has to do with developing awareness and new ideas, then practicing them. That's why God created families to be a place of growth and development. Understanding the conscience provides more tools for accomplishing some of the goals every family has. Kids become more sensitive to internal promptings of the conscience and the Holy Spirit, and maturity and responsibility are the result.

8

Kids Taking Initiative

Courage without a strong conscience can
lead children into all kinds of calamity.

You could hear the frustration in Tamela's voice. "I feel like
I'm a crazy person sometimes. I have four kids between
the ages of seven and sixteen, and they leave things all over the
house. Several times a day I have to stop and make them pick
things up and put them away, but just an hour later the house is
a mess again. I don't like it that I'm always nagging and yelling at
them, but I don't know what else to do. I wish they could just do
it without being told."

Tamela's words could have come out of the mouth of many
moms and dads today. It's encouraging to a parent's heart when
kids take initiative on their own. The preschooler who picks up
some trash and puts it into the trash can, the elementary child
who loads the dishwasher without being asked, and the teen
who remembers it's Tuesday and takes the recycling down to the
street all have one thing in common. They saw a need and took
initiative to address it. On the other hand, little benefit is gained

from the conscience if children receive a prompting and don't know how or don't have the character to respond to it.

Tamela was pleased with the solutions we gave her. As she started to implement them, she saw changes in her kids and in herself. As Tamela was willing to make some adjustments in the way she worked with her kids, it made a huge difference in their initiative and in their relationships together. We'll share her strategy and some more ideas in this chapter.

Teaching Kids to Take Initiative

One of the most important heart qualities children can develop is initiative, and parents can do a lot to facilitate its strength. Initiative is simply taking action without being asked. However, to take initiative, one must have three things: a sensitivity to internal promptings, courage or obligation to respond, and wisdom to take action appropriately. After all, an internal urge to do something may come from the heart, but that doesn't make it a wise thing to do.

> One of the most important heart qualities children can develop is initiative, and parents can do a lot to facilitate its strength.

Children develop greater sensitivity to internal promptings when parents, teachers, and other leaders help raise awareness. When Samuel heard his name called in the middle of the night, he simply thought it was Eli, the priest, calling him. Only after Eli told Samuel that the voice was from God was Samuel able to listen to the Lord. Eli instructed Samuel, "Go and lie down, and if he calls you [again], say, Speak, LORD, for your servant is listening" (1 Samuel 3:9). Samuel did what Eli said, and in that moment began to hear the voice of God in his life.

One dad asked his eight-year-old son, "Does God speak to you?" It's surprising how many Christian kids say no. His son also said no, but after thinking for a moment, he changed his mind and said, "I mean, yes."

Dad used that question to help raise awareness of the internal promptings of the Holy Spirit and of the conscience. He responded by saying, "You're right. God speaks to kids through the Bible, through parents, through other leaders and authorities, through inner promptings, and through prayer. But you have to listen in order to hear what God has to say. Furthermore, God uses the promptings of the conscience to make us aware of things at times. When you're sensitive to the conscience, good things happen."

Over the next few days, they had a fun interaction together. Dad, at random times, said, "What is God saying to you now?" They talked about how God doesn't just speak at church or when we open the Bible. He can speak at any time, and we must be ready to listen to what he has to say. Of course, sometimes it's hard to know if it's the Holy Spirit talking, the conscience prompting, or just our own imaginations giving us an idea. That's why it's important to spend a lot of time with God's Word to make sure that what we're hearing is actually from God.

Developing initiative in kids helps foster the courage and confidence they need to see problems in life and do something about them. When children believe they have a solution and can actually solve a problem, they're often willing to get involved in doing so. Of course, some kids are afraid to make mistakes. Those kids need help translating mistakes into learning experiences. Only those who are willing to take the risk of failure are able to obtain success. When parents make taking initiative part of their training, kids start to do it on their own.

We first helped Tamela understand herself. Inside her own heart she would come to a point of reaction. That point was very important because it was an internal signal that something was wrong and needed a plan. Her plan of yelling and nagging wasn't working. Her first task was to gain control of herself at that moment and appropriate godly peace in her heart. The pressure to react needed to be met with an internal plan of Holy Spirit control.

Next, Tamela needed to start working on each of her children individually. Each one needed a plan for being more thoughtful and careful about things around the house. She decided to start with her twelve-year-old. "Son, I don't like the way I've been responding to you about leaving your stuff around the house. I'd like to make some changes, and I need your help. In fact, this new plan will benefit you, too, because it will help you be more considerate of others." Together they developed some ways that he could jog his memory. One of the ideas was to ask a question every time he passed through a doorway: "Did I leave anything undone behind me?"

Through practice, Mom helped her son make some internal changes. She explained it this way: "I'm not asking you to want to clean up. I'm asking you to clean up even though you don't feel like it. One of the signs of maturity is when you do the right thing even when the desire isn't there."

Sometimes parents say, "I wish I could get my kids to want to do the things they are supposed to do." But is that always reasonable? After all, look at us as adults. We often do what's right in spite of our desires. The real goal should be that our kids learn to do what they are supposed to do even when they don't want to. That's maturity in action. The child who completes homework before playing, cleans up his own mess, or lets someone else go first demonstrates inner strength to overcome selfish tendencies to do otherwise.

Parents can help their children develop this inner character by teaching them how to work hard, take on responsibility, and finish tasks. It may be easier at times to do it yourself because it's more efficient, but your investment in your child will pay off immensely down the road.

Kids Need Wisdom

Some children have more initiative than is helpful at times. They barge in with little concern for the consequences. Lindsay is eight and tends to speak her mind. She sees something that's wrong and points it out, with no obvious concern for the other person who is listening. She apparently believes that if she's right, then she can point it out. Unfortunately, Lindsay doesn't know how best to respond to the internal promptings she experiences. Kids like Lindsay need wisdom to know how best to respond. God uses the term *wisdom* for situations such as these. The Hebrew word for wisdom gives us insight into its importance. *Hokmah* literally means "skill in life." Those skills are important and teach children when it's appropriate to interrupt, how to balance relationship with truth, and what to do when disappointment clouds the picture. Kids learn wisdom through teaching and experience. Both are important.

> Kids learn wisdom through teaching and experience. Both are important.

Teaching provides practical situations where kids see life challenges met with skillful responses. Experience teaches children how to learn from mistakes and to remember things that worked well. Wisdom takes years to develop and requires humility and a teachable attitude.

If you realize that wisdom is often gained through experience, you'll be more likely to allow your children the freedom to make mistakes. Affirmation of children in the learning process is strategic for helping them develop the internal strength to take risks as they get older. Of course, some children are natural risk takers, and their lack of wisdom could lead them into all kinds of problems. It's important not to allow children to play with evil or to make a mistake that might have huge consequences in their lives.

Internal motivation is not always good. Many things are going on inside the human heart. Kids are motivated by desires and emotions. The role of the conscience and the Holy Spirit is to provide guidance for the heart and keep it moving in the right direction. The goal isn't to simply get kids to do things on their own. The challenge of parenting is to train kids to be internally motivated to do the *right* things, not just *anything*. Building a healthy quality of initiative is directly related to conscience development. Training about right and wrong helps curb unhelpful desires. Inner promptings provide the clues to children that they should either take action or not. The conscience needs training, and you will have many opportunities in daily interaction to weave conscience-related truths into your interaction with your kids.

One good way to teach children about the internal promptings of the conscience and initiative is through heroes. In fact, heroes are characterized by the same four promptings that come from every person's conscience. They do what's right, deal with wrongs, are honest, and care about others. Since children love heroes, it's an appropriate way to teach them more about how God picks people to do great things in life.

A Hero in the Small Things

Consider the life of David. Of course, we know that David became a public hero when he killed Goliath. But it didn't start there.

Rather, we see him being a hero in the small things of life when he was a child. For example, he practiced his musical instrument, much like many children today, so he was able to get a job playing it in the palace. He took care of the sheep, as kids today take care of animals around the house. And David was responsible enough for his dad to send him on an errand, delivering cheeses to the commanding officer at the battle-front. David practiced hero-like qualities long before he was publicly recognized as a hero.

> David practiced hero-like qualities long before he was publicly recognized as a hero.

Kids can do the same thing. When they see what needs to be done and they do it without being asked, they're taking the initiative that God will use in their lives both now and later. It starts in the small things of life. You might say to your daughter, "Go stand in the doorway to the living room and tell me three things you see that are out of place." After she identifies them, you might say, "Okay, let's see if you can fix them." When she's done, you'll want to point out to her that she not only sees things that need to be done but she knows how to fix them. Those are the same qualities a hero has.

You can encourage initiative in children in the common, everyday tasks of family life. Take the process of giving instructions, for example. If your son's chore is feeding the dog, then you might transfer responsibility to your son for not only doing the job but also remembering to do it. That requires initiative. He can use a number of reminder techniques, just as adults do. It may be some form of alarm, a sticky note, or a check box on the calendar. It would be best if you didn't tell him what reminder system to use, but rather asked him to develop it. Now you're training him to develop systems to help him remember to do what's right. Then you keep an eye out to make sure the system is working. If the alarm goes off at 8:00 a.m. and he forgets, you might draw attention to the alarm instead of the task by saying, "Didn't I hear your alarm go off?" By pointing out the cue instead of the task, you're working the system inside his heart. Now you are fostering internal motivation in the daily grind of life, where kids need to see it the most.

Another way to foster initiative in children is to occasionally give them choices instead of direct instructions. You might say to a young child, "Would you rather I read this book or that one?" Or, "Would you like celery or apples to dip into the peanut butter?" For an older child, you might say, "Did you want to mow the lawn before lunch when it's cooler or after lunch when it's warmer?" Notice that these kinds of choices aren't so open-ended that they allow children to run the family. They simply guide children by allowing them to be part of the decision-making process.

Some well-meaning parents overdo choices and end up allowing kids too much leadership in the home. Mom finds herself cooking several lunches for her family or ends up going to a fast-food restaurant to please a child instead of taking stronger leadership in the home. Unfortunately, those children often become demanding, expecting that others should do what they want.

> Some well-meaning parents overdo choices and end up allowing kids too much leadership in the home.

On the other hand, some parents overemphasize obedience, and their authoritarian approach to parenting squelches any initiative a child might have. A careful balance is in order here. Limited choices often provide children a sense of initiative because they force the child to make a decision and stick with it. If Grant opts for eggs, he can't change his mind when he sees them and say that he wants pancakes instead. When he chooses baseball instead of soccer and feels the pressure, he can't drop out. Making decisions is one thing. Sticking to them is another, and it teaches children to consider their ways carefully before the decision is made.

The Ten-Dollar Predicament

Dwayne and Charles each had ten dollars to spend on vacation. Dwayne spent his at the first opportunity, while Charles was less eager. Dwayne was disappointed as he saw more and more options of things he could have spent his money on. Dad and Mom were firm with Dwayne, although it was hard for them when they saw some things they knew Dwayne would really like. The lesson learned is an important one that will help Dwayne over time consider his options before he makes his decisions. Dwayne was learning to evaluate his internal motivations. The heart's desires often provide impulses to act, limiting the future choices one might have.

Allowing children to take initiative means that parents must be willing to accept and know how to respond to mistakes. Children will at times get hurt, miss out, or offend someone. How parents respond is important. Correction isn't always necessary, because the child is learning from life. The parent then can respond as a coach, demonstrating empathy and counsel. When five-year-old Jeremiah tried riding the skateboard, his parents praised his courage to try something new. When he gained some confidence, his silliness resulted in a fall. Instead of running over hysterically to see if he was okay, Mom waited for a moment to see what would happen. Her son looked at her to see how she would respond. She simply shrugged her shoulders and said, "Looks like you're doing great. Maybe a little too much silliness. Go ahead and try again." Jeremiah seemed to need that affirmation from Mom as permission to move ahead and continued to play.

You can build a child's sense of confidence by giving opportunities to succeed that involve risk. For example, you might allow a child to carry the pie to the other room, crack the eggs for breakfast, or pour milk. Invariably children will make mistakes. How you respond is strategic. Recovering from mistakes is an important part of developing confidence and increases a child's willingness to initiate.

Using Correction to Provide Wisdom

Parents correct children every day, and how they do it can increase or decrease a child's initiative. For example, when a parent separates the action from the person, the child learns that he isn't bad just because he did something wrong. He is still loved, competent, and capable, but needs to change his behavior. On the other hand, parents who use anger to punish their kids reduce a child's willingness to take risks or try new things. Look for ways to affirm the child when correcting to maximize the discipline process.

When you have to say no or set limits for children, it's often helpful to share reasons behind the rules or convictions that drive your decision. Parents who are in the habit of saying no a lot may limit a child's initiative in life. Those kids tend to wait until told what they can do instead of initiating, and then fail when trying to move forward.

Here's another area, though, where parents can overdo it. If every time you say no you have to give a reason to justify your answer, kids may tend to argue. Sometimes children simply need to accept no as an answer. Even we, as adults, must do that at times, so it's not unreasonable to require that children accept no without a reason. When possible, however, it's helpful to share values and information so kids learn why. It helps them in their future decision making.

In addition, it's best to teach children a wise appeal approach when they want to challenge a no answer from an authority. A wise appeal gives kids a practical tool for taking initiative when they get a no. A wise appeal has three parts. First, start with acknowledging the parent's concern by saying something like, "I understand you want me to . . . because . . ." Then express your own desire by saying something like, "But I have a problem with that because . . ." End by giving an alternative that somehow offers a solution for the parent and for the child in the form of a new idea or compromise of some sort.

> Sometimes children simply need to accept no as an answer.

Parents are much more willing to revisit a decision if children approach their appeal in a respectful way. Furthermore, parents are more eager to accept a new idea that seems to consider their concerns. Ingrid asked for a snack, and Mom said no. Ingrid came back a couple of minutes later and said, "Mom, I understand you don't want me to have a snack because sometimes I don't eat my dinner and we're eating in a half hour. I have a problem with that because I didn't have much lunch at school today and I'm really hungry. So could I please have half of an apple? I'll be sure to eat my food at dinnertime."

Mom was impressed with her daughter's appeal and granted her request. The wise appeal, learned at home, can be used with other leaders and authorities as well. Coaches and teachers are often open to an appeal made with respect. Children, however, must be able to respond well to a no answer. If the authority still says no, it's important to submit without a bad attitude. The wise appeal is just another way to teach initiative in children through simple relational routines in family life.

Goals Help Kids Think More Broadly About Life

It's helpful for children to develop goals. Those then become targets that motivate children to take initiative in various areas of their lives. It may be a character goal, such as becoming more patient with a sibling or more self-controlled with anger. It may be a skill goal, like learning how to ride a bike or read a chapter book. Or it may be a task goal, such as memorizing math facts or cleaning up a room. When you allow kids to come up with goals, you'll adjust to a more coaching role as they move toward their objective. You might ask a child, "What are your goals for this summer?" (or this Christmas, or on this vacation, or even for today). Then share your own personal goals by way of illustration.

Kids also learn valuable lessons in the area of initiative when they volunteer to help others without getting paid. It might be helping in the children's ministry at church, raking the neighbor's leaves, or taking on some kind of service project. The child develops confidence and experiences the satisfaction of helping others. Many children today don't think much about others and can become rather self-focused in their approach to life. By being required to perform some kind of service, kids learn to think past themselves and experience the benefits of their work.

As you help your child develop initiative, especially in response to internal promptings, you're forming the basis for responsibility and maturity. Kids learn that they have influence on the way things turn out in life and aren't just victims of life. Furthermore, when children learn to respond to the conscience, true moral development takes place. Kids learn to take a stand for righteousness, develop their own convictions, and refuse to engage in dishonest activity. As you raise the awareness of the conscience and encourage children to take action, you'll help them apply the conscience to everyday decisions of life.

9

What About
Consequences?

In order for consequences to work, they must
prompt dialogue in the child's heart that says,
"I think my current plan isn't working for me."

K elly was exasperated. "I've tried everything with my twelve-
year-old son. Nothing seems to motivate Mike. We've taken
away most everything he has. He still doesn't change. We've
grounded him. It doesn't faze him. He doesn't care. We don't know
what else to do."

As we worked with Kelly, she realized that her overempha-
sis on external rewards and punishment had been ineffective
at training her son's heart. Her son was strong-willed, and that
meant external motivators wouldn't work as a day-to-day strategy with her son. Although they seemed to produce results at
first, the effects of rewards and punishment faded over time. In
fact, he seemed to become resistant to her approach.

What Kelly and her son needed was a completely different
plan that emphasized heart change instead of just behavior. As

Kelly made adjustments, so did Mike, and remarkable improvement took place. But Kelly was back in our office two months later with a very important question. "What is a healthy way to use consequences with kids?"

That's a good question, and many of the thoughts shared in this chapter will provide greater insight into ways to use consequences within a heart-based approach to build internal motivation. If the heart isn't changing, you'll likely want to evaluate your approach. There are many good and godly ways to raise children. Just because one technique worked with another child doesn't mean it will work with yours. Tailoring a plan for each child will consider specific needs and challenges, resulting in more effective parenting strategies.

Remember, the goal of parenting isn't just to make kids happy. Those whose primary goal is to make their children happy often raise selfish children. Kids need firmness in order to move away from their weaknesses. Many kids are very comfortable with laziness, emotional outbursts, or disrespect. They need loving parents who are willing to set firm boundaries to help them move forward toward the goal.

> **Firmness helps draw a line inside a child's heart defining right and wrong.**

Firmness helps draw a line inside a child's heart defining right and wrong. The conscience needs training, and firmness clarifies the basis upon which the conscience draws its information.

The goal of correction is heart change, and it's important to realize that consequences aren't always necessary for that heart change to take place. Furthermore, choosing the best consequence for a particular situation can be challenging. Many parents tend to narrow their repertoire of consequences to a few, or they have a favorite one that they use over and over again.

Taking away a privilege, going to bed early, or grounding a child are just a few parental favorites. Unfortunately, some parents even use anger as their primary consequence, punishing a child with harshness and distance.

It's like the one-tooled handyman. Every time something breaks, he has only one tool, a hammer. If a pipe leaks, he hits it with a hammer; if the air conditioner doesn't work, he hits it with a hammer. If the window is broken, he tries to fix it with a hammer. Of course that's absurd, yet many parents take that kind of approach to parenting. They have one tool, whatever their favorite might be, and that's what they tend to use in every discipline situation. Furthermore, when the only tool you have is a hammer, every problem looks like a nail. Children are more complex than that. Their problems require a strategy for consistent growth to take place.

If moms and dads are going to mold their children's hearts, they need to do some planning, and they need to choose the right tools. Parents need a toolbox of consequences to help them work on the various challenges they face with their kids. But consequences are just a part of what we call "discipline." So before we get into specifics about individual tools, keep these facts in mind.

First, consequences are part of a bigger plan. *Discipline* means "to teach." Children are in the God-given process of growing up. Consequences are only a part of a good teaching plan.

Second, the goal of correction is not justice, but training. Some parents have a "chart mentality" when it comes to discipline. "You did this, so you deserve that." This kind of approach rarely touches a child's heart.

Third, discipline requires patience and firmness over time. Children rarely change quickly. Most issues require that you develop a plan and work that plan with your children for quite a while before they develop the character necessary to continue on their own.

Fourth, consequences help clarify for kids the line between right and wrong. That line, drawn over and over in a child's heart, clarifies messages that the conscience provides. Consequences done well contribute to conscience development.

And last, when you think consequences, you have to think strategy. Plan consequences for maximum impact. Don't give them impulsively. Don't fall into the trap of reactive discipline.

Consequences are one tool to motivate change. They can make the child's current plan uncomfortable and motivate him or her to respond differently.

A Toolbox of Consequences

Let's look at several types of consequences and evaluate how to use them in a way that will contribute to the development of internal motivation.

Natural consequences are the normal results of the choices your children make. They allow kids to receive correction from life. Although it's often easier to learn from teaching or advice, some kids seem to need to learn experientially. With natural consequences, you don't have to be the bad guy because you're not giving the consequence; life is. As a result, natural consequences are your friend if you know how to respond when they happen.

When Karen plays rough with the cat, for example, she gets scratched. Bill leaves his soccer shoes out on the porch, and they get wet in the rain. Rick forgets to take his coat to the park, and he's cold. Jill is silly on the skateboard and falls off and skins her elbow. Jimmy doesn't eat his lunch, and then he's hungry.

Parents make an important choice when they see natural

consequences happening with their children. They either align themselves with the child or they align themselves with the consequence. If you take the side of the consequence, then you say things like, "I told you that was going to happen." Or, "See? If you'd just listen to me . . ."

The key to gaining the most out of natural consequences is to align yourself with your child by expressing empathy. "Ouch! I'll bet that hurt. Come here and let me see." Genuine empathy places you on your child's side as a counselor or coach. Be careful not to launch into a lecture when natural consequences hit home. Sometimes you might make a comment to help the child connect the consequence to a life lesson, but be careful that it doesn't appear to be a documentary. If you do, you'll likely lose the benefit, and the child may resist receiving the lesson.

Natural consequences are your friend if you know how to respond when they happen.

Children often develop internal motivation when the experience of life demonstrates what works and what doesn't. Some parents get quite frustrated with their children who won't listen to instruction or advice, and they throw up their hands and say, "I give up. He'll just have to learn the hard way." Sometimes allowing natural consequences makes an important impact. However, some kids don't respond to them either, so other tools from the training toolbox will be necessary.

Kelly had an important decision to make. Mike left his homework assignment at home. Mom found the paper on the table just as she was about to go out the door. She asked herself, "Should I let him learn by experience or should I help him out?" Kelly had learned to evaluate these kinds of situations, recognizing that the answer depended on several factors. What does Mike need to learn? On the one hand, if she was trying to teach him not to be careless about turning in his homework, she might take advantage of the forgotten assignment to allow the consequence to bring a painful reminder. On the other hand, a family is a place where we take care of one another and help one another out. Each member in need can rely on others to take up the slack. If that's the principle she wanted to emphasize, then she would take the forgotten homework to school with a smile.

Jesus used natural consequences with Peter in Matthew 14. When Peter wanted to come out on the water, Jesus simply said, "Come," and allowed Peter to learn from experience the importance of keeping his eyes focused on the Savior. Also, in Luke 22, when Peter denied Christ, Jesus didn't give a lecture or a time-out. It was just the look in the Master's eyes that caused Peter to go out and weep bitterly. Why? Because the natural consequence of lying is damaged relationship.

Although natural consequences can be a great teacher, they must be abandoned when people or property are in danger or when they take too long to be effective. In those cases you might use *logical consequences* instead to communicate a similar message about life.

> The success of logical consequences rests partly on the parent's ability to empathize with the child.

Rick, age five, and Tom, age eight, are digging holes in the front yard with a shovel, damaging the lawn. Dad steps in and stops them from digging and, as a consequence, requires that they rake the leaves into piles. It's a logical consequence because destroying the yard is replaced with the task of improving it.

Mindy, age fourteen, left her favorite coat at the gym again. Mom retrieves the coat but tells Mindy she can't wear it for a week and must wear her old one instead. It's a logical consequence because actually losing the coat would mean not wearing it ever again.

Tony, age nine, steals a pack of candy from the store. Mom takes Tony back to the store to ask for forgiveness. It's a logical consequence because people who steal eventually get caught and have to face the situation with humility. Mom's just speeding up the process.

Monte, age four, continually slams his door when he's angry. Dad decides that he'll remove the door from Monte's room for a while. It's a logical consequence because eventually slamming a door means that you'd lose it because it would break.

In each of these cases, the goal of the logical consequence is to teach a life lesson in hopes that the children will develop an internal desire to adjust the way they live. The success of logical consequences rests partly on the parent's ability to empathize with the child. "Oh, I'm sorry you did that; now you're going to have to be disciplined."

In John 13:4–10, Jesus got up to wash the disciples' feet. Peter didn't want to participate, telling Jesus no. Jesus responded with a logical consequence that said, "Then you can't be part of me." Peter, realizing the significance of the washing, changed his mind and invited Jesus to wash his whole body. Peter got the message and changed his heart. Jesus used the warning of a logical consequence to teach Peter the important lesson.

Another tool in the toolbox is the *loss of a privilege*. Sometimes children must lose some of their privileges in order to recognize the importance of changing. For example, Kari, age sixteen, talks on the phone for long periods of time, disregarding parental warnings, so Mom takes her phone away. Kari no longer has free access to the phone but must get permission from Mom to use it.

Wendy, age seven, is disrespectful to Mom, so Mom tells Wendy she can't go to her friend's house to play today. Tim, age ten, procrastinates in doing his homework, so Dad tells him he won't be able to watch the baseball game on TV until he finishes the assignment.

Some parents struggle with taking away privileges because they want their children to enjoy the things that are often associated with a particular age or stage of life. But when children aren't yet mature enough to handle those privileges, and parents give them anyway, the kids flounder in irresponsibility.

Learning to drive, having a cell phone, and playing on the computer are all privileges that require a certain level of maturity, not just being a particular age. Parents need to evaluate if a child is really mature enough to handle these things, not simply rely on what other children of the same age are doing. The child who doesn't have the character yet needs fewer privileges because privilege and responsibility go together.

Jesus taught his disciples about responsibility in Matthew 25:14–29 by telling them the parable of the landowner who left talents in his stewards' hands while he was gone. When he returned to check on their work, he discovered that two were responsible and one was not. To the faithful stewards he said, "Because you've been faithful over a few things, I will make you ruler over many things."

To the lazy servant he said, "Even the little you have will be taken from you." That's the same principle parents teach their children when they remove or give privileges. Responsibility is a prerequisite for the privileges children want to enjoy.

The key to building internal motivation with this form of consequence is to have children earn back the privilege. Parents often make the mistake of taking away a privilege for a certain length of time, saying something like, "You're going to lose your video game for a week." That's a common behavior-modification strategy but often misses the heart of the child. Here's why. By taking away a privilege for a set period of time, you remove an important ingredient from your discipline: hope. Kelly realized that Mike would just give up internally and say, "Why should I change? There's nothing I can do to get my video game back. I just need to wait it out for a week."

Kelly realized that she could use the loss of a privilege to build internal motivation by avoiding a time limit and instead requiring that Mike earn the privilege back. "I'll give your video game back when you show me that you can have a positive attitude when I give you an instruction. I'm ready to practice whenever you are." Now Mike was motivated to improve a pattern, and Kelly was contributing to a change of heart.

> The key to building internal motivation with a loss of privileges is to have children earn back the privilege.

Allowing children to earn back privileges gives them hope, and it increases the number of times you can use that consequence to teach and correct. At that moment you are using the consequence to build new patterns. Sometimes parents think that a big consequence will increase learning, but often it's the smaller giving and taking of privileges that helps children change.

Because some children lack the self-control necessary to be successful in life, they need *more parental control*, another tool in the consequence toolbox. For example, Pete, age five, is touching things at the museum, so Dad requires Pete to hold his hand for a while. Al, age eight, can't practice the piano for more than five minutes without distraction. So Mom sits with Al for thirty minutes each afternoon during his practice sessions.

Parents often don't like the consequence of more parental control because it means more time and energy on their part. Sure, it would be easier to just sit back and watch kids grow, but the reality is that they often need close supervision and instruction.

More parental control is difficult when children become teenagers. Just when you thought you could have a little less parental involvement and a little more free time, you're called upon to get more involved again. Martha, age thirteen, is failing at school because she isn't completing her homework. Mom gets more involved, requiring her daughter to show her assignments each afternoon. Mom checks Martha's work and increases direct communication with the teacher.

Some parents make the mistake of using natural consequences when children are failing. They say, "Fine. Just let him fail. Maybe then he'll learn." Unfortunately, only the exceptionally motivated child is able to break the cycle and begin to succeed after failing. Most kids in those situations need more parental control to see that, yes, they can succeed; otherwise they develop an identity as a failure.

> Some parents make the mistake of using natural consequences when children are failing.

If you want your children to be successful, sometimes you have to get more involved in their lives, not less involved. It's hard, time consuming, and takes a lot more energy, but this is often the consequence children need to get back on track. Using the consequence of more parental control means that children must report in often and parents monitor closely, bringing more accountability. Parents even get involved in doing the task sometimes. With more parental control children learn that they can do the job and that they have what it takes to succeed.

On the other hand, some parents overuse more parental control. For example, when a child dawdles at mealtime, a natural consequence may be more effective, for instance, simply saying to the child, "Lunch is over in five minutes. Eat whatever you want, because the next meal is dinner." Too much emphasis on more parental control can weaken relationship and sometimes reduces internal motivation. Too much emphasis on natural consequences can result in children who become discouraged or who simply stop trying. A careful balance between the two is important.

An interesting biblical study in more parental control leads us to the work God did in the lives of the Israelites as they left Egypt. He led them with a cloud by day and a pillar of fire by night. He fed them with manna and gave them strict guidelines for how they should live their new lives. They needed time to learn how to manage their new freedom.

When they reached the promised land, they proved that they weren't ready to trust God to face the giants in the land. So God allowed them to wander in the wilderness with more parental control for forty years. When they finally returned to the Jordan River, they were ready to trust God. They had learned what they needed to learn. So, after they entered the new land, God stopped the manna and, over time, used prophets to guide them. God reduced the parental control as their faith grew.

Teenagers yearn for freedom and independence, but the dangers and risks multiply exponentially at this stage of life. Often teens need closer monitoring and greater accountability than they did just a few years earlier. More parental control means pursuing teenagers and staying closely involved in their lives. That can be difficult given the many commitments and challenges parents face.

More parental control is like a Jell-O mold for kids. While their character is weak, parents provide the structures of life. As children grow more in their self-control, parents are able to remove their own control, leaving children to stand on their own. Some parents make the mistake of allowing their teens far more control of their lives than is helpful. At this stage more parental control is often necessary to keep kids on track as life gets more complicated. More parental control is a useful consequence when children need help to be successful. It's often the consequence needed when a child is doing poorly at school or struggling with managing money. As kids improve, parents can slowly remove the control, allowing the child's self-control to gradually take over.

One consequence that is often overlooked yet is quite powerful for building new patterns has to do with *practicing the right thing*. Some children need to practice over and over again. In fact, the consequence for a negative pattern of behavior may be to practice doing what's right for a time.

Richie, age seven, is mean to his younger sister. He appears to enjoy being mean, and no consequences seem to have an effect. Mom decided to have Richie think of and do two kind things for his sister. Mom repeats this consequence a couple times a day.

Kim, age four, runs away from her mom in the grocery store. As a consequence, Mom practices a "come when you're called" rule several times an hour throughout the day.

Bert, age fourteen, has a bad attitude when given an instruction. Dad tells Bert that he has five jobs for Saturday morning cleanup, and Bert will have to do at least two, but may have to do up to five based on how well he can respond to the instructions.

Many children who have bad attitudes or who are resistant to instruction or correction need to learn how to work harder. When kids learn to work hard, they develop perseverance, confidence, and the ability to take on an assignment with determination to succeed. If your children seem to have a hard time with their level of work, maybe it's time to increase the pressure. In the end this could have a very positive effect.

Romans 5:3–4 says that "suffering produces perseverance; perseverance, character; and character, hope." Many children lack hope. They become easily discouraged and give up. The solution is to develop character, and that often comes from perseverance that in turn comes from suffering. Increasing our children's workload can be that "suffering" that they need to develop the strength to carry them through life's challenges.

Building internal motivation requires training. It requires that you think more broadly about consequences so that your thinking incorporates more than just nega-

> Romans 5:3–4 says that "suffering produces perseverance; perseverance, character; and character, hope."

tive ways to change behavior. Those deterrents are helpful in motivating children to change, but many children need the continual practice of doing the right thing.

Putting Together Your Plan

Consequences are often a way of getting your child's attention and providing an external motivation to change. They are a wake-up call that says, "You can't continue to live this way." Some children stubbornly hold on to faulty operating principles in their hearts. They continue to react with anger, deception, bad attitudes, or resistance. Consequences chip away at hard hearts, bumping against foolish thinking with doses of reality. The goal of an external consequence is to build internal motivation to change.

The key word to consider when evaluating consequences is *strategy*. People change for two reasons. Either life becomes uncomfortable or they gain a vision for something better. Parents can work hard to build vision in their kids, but often it's the uncomfortable reality of consequences that begins the process of heart change. Consequences create a crisis of sorts in a child's heart.

As he did with Jonah and Paul, God uses life-changing events in our lives to adjust what we believe and how we operate. The small consequences of day-to-day discipline make significant inroads over time. You may feel as if you're not seeing the change you'd like to see, but hang in there. Anyone who has worked a garden knows the tremendous labor required before fruit results. Patience and hard work pay off over time as we do the heart work of parenting.

10

Putting the Conscience to Work Outside the Home

The conscience prompts action, but kids
need coaching to help them know how
to react to challenging situations.

Children face conscience issues every day. Nancy's friends won't allow Amy to eat at their lunch table. Nancy experiences an internal struggle. She wants to include Amy, but she doesn't want to oppose her friends, lest she, too, be barred from the group.

Charlie kicks the ball, and it goes over the fence at school. He can see the ball and almost reach it, but it seems that the only way to get it is to jump over the fence. No one has ever told him not to go over the fence, but something about it just doesn't seem right. His conscience plays a role as he considers his options.

Romy feels uncomfortable because the rule is to get home by dark, but he and his friend just finished building the skateboard ramp and haven't cleaned up yet. What he chooses to do in this situation is important, and the conscience will play a role in his decision making.

Preparing Kids to Live Responsibly When They Aren't with You

When children are with parents, Dad and Mom often guide their kids to make the best choices, but when those children are outside the home, they must rely on the training they've received to face the challenges of life. "Do I take another brownie or leave it for someone else?" "Should I clean up as I go or clean up at the end?" "Do I try to influence the situation toward what seems to be the right choice or try to fit in for now and see if it works out?" These choices aren't easy ones and require that children not only have rules to guide their thinking but also have the ability to think through the options and weigh out various factors.

Kids often meet challenges that pit various parts of the conscience against one another. Violating a rule to help someone else is a challenge for anyone. In business, it's either called a breach of conduct if the rule has moral implications, or good customer service when that rule seems not to apply in a situation. Children often need help to understand the difference.

> Kids often meet challenges that pit various parts of the conscience against one another.

You'll want to do some conscience training to empower children to approach life's challenges outside the home. That means providing them with clear values, convictions, and family rules, and then giving them a chance to test them out in real situations. They'll learn to think independently, and have opportunities to fail and to receive honest but compassionate feedback. As they learn from victories and mistakes, kids develop a confidence for handling all kinds of situations in life.

You might start by talking to your kids at home about potential situations and helping them evaluate the options. For example, you may ask your six-year-old, "If you're over at a friend's house and your friend does this, what should you do?" Then present several different scenarios. For instance, you could say the friend

- burps without saying, "Excuse me."
- takes one of your Lego pieces to build his project.
- hits you because you took back your Lego piece.
- lies and tells his mom that he had the Lego piece first.
- tells you that he stole the Lego set from the store.

For each scenario, ask the child, "What would you do: ignore it, confront him, or report it?" The discussion that follows is helpful because of the reasons behind the decision, not just the decision itself.

Or you might ask a teenager a similar question by saying, "When someone is doing the wrong thing at school, how do you know when to ignore it, confront the person, or report it to the authorities? What are some examples?"

It's these types of questions that get kids thinking at home before they find themselves in real situations. Children of all ages need to learn how to balance the rules, values, and convictions you've taught them. It's often the experiences of life that move external rules into the heart to become convictions. Parents teach about the values of honesty, compassion, justice, and respect for others, but knowing what to do when those convictions are violated in life requires insight and wisdom. Kids need to learn how to practice what they believe. Take the subject of justice, for example. Some children have a high value for justice, and when someone crosses that line, they're quick to get upset. That can be a valuable asset at times, but other times a detriment. For example, when one friend treats your other friend unfairly, how do you respond? What if you're the one being mistreated? What if you feel that a teacher is mistreating you? Each of those situations involves an uncomfortable feeling in the conscience that needs a response, but other values, such as graciousness and respect for authority, must be considered as well.

Faith and the Conscience

Faith plays an important role in conscience formation and the ability to respond with internal motivation to life's challenges. Having courage to stand up for what's right, or initiative to help a hurting friend, or self-control to avoid retaliating when offended are all opportunities to practice one's personal faith. That's why it's so important to read God's Word with your children, share biblical truths, and teach kids about biblical characters who faced challenges. That teaching forms the basis for how children will decide for themselves what they will do when they face various situations.

Talking to kids about their experiences often produces opportunities to dialogue about convictions and decision making. But be careful that you don't pounce too quickly and enter into a lecture mode. Kids benefit from questions too. But sometimes a little lecture is just what a child needs and even wants. One teen boy, reflecting on his mom's words, said, "You used to tell me all the time to think about how I would feel if someone else did that to me. That helped me as I related to others and is an important factor now in my choices."

The goal is to help children catch the truth, and sometimes

a less direct approach works better. A question may help a child come to a conclusion on her own, making that truth more relevant and real. Simply giving children the answer to a problem may not be as powerful as helping them reach a conclusion through guided conversation.

When Kids Resist

Some children resist conscience training. Sometimes it's because their desire to have what they want is so strong that moral factors seem unimportant to them. Other kids have a highly emotional personality, making it harder to execute logical decisions on the spot. When desires or emotions become too dominant in a child's life, quite a bit of work is required to increase the role of values and convictions in decision making. When children tend to be self-absorbed instead of others-centered, it's harder for them to make a decision about what's right.

Furthermore, some kids seem to be bent on doing the wrong thing. It's troubling for a parent to see a child cut corners and violate family values to accomplish a goal or get something he or she wants. Those kids need more accountability and more external leadership in their lives. Giving a lot of freedom to a child with poor moral development is rarely helpful. That freedom only serves to provide more opportunity to practice doing what's wrong. This child needs some significant work to retrain internal motivation.

> Giving a lot of freedom to a child with poor moral development is rarely helpful.

The child who has weak moral character needs more oversight. Parents must exercise caution when evaluating requests that place children in situations where supervision is low. It's often best to provide opportunities to have friends over to your house or activities that you're involved in so you can guide and monitor things. When the child does go somewhere else, it's often helpful for parents to check in with the authorities there. Talking to teachers at school about your child's need for limit setting, or making sure a parent is home and aware when your child goes over to a friend's house, is important.

Red flags should go up when kids ask to hang out after dark, want to go to a party, or attend a sleepover. It's amazing how quickly kids can get into trouble when they have a bent toward doing the wrong thing and there's no adult on duty. Kids can easily discover evil today, and if they're looking for trouble, they'll usually find it. Those kids need a lot of training, supervision, and limits to make it through childhood without doing significant damage to themselves and others.

The Importance of Boundaries

Enforcing firm boundaries is a positive way to contribute to conscience development. Even a child who tends to push the limits or go outside of the boundaries to find satisfaction or pleasure learns from a firm approach exactly where the boundary lines are. Over time, with much prayer and perseverance, those children learn that there's a line between right and wrong, and continually crossing that line produces consequences and wearies the soul. Some children take longer than others to choose right responses simply because it's the right thing to do, so it's important to persevere and hang in there.

When parents continually point out the need to choose good friends and make right choices, and then allow children to experience the consequences of poor decisions, children learn. It's always easier to learn from someone else's experience or from good teaching, but some kids seem to need to learn on their own by trying things that don't work. Your job as a parent is to make their self-directed experiment as real and as clear as possible. Experiencing painful consequences is important for some kids to get the message that doing the wrong thing isn't worth it.

When the police showed up at Sharon's house, she was alarmed. Apparently her son, Terrance, and his friend Jules damaged the neighbor's fence by throwing rocks at a target they'd set up on it. Sharon had to make an important choice. Because her son tended to be mischievous, she decided to allow the police officer to speak directly to her son. She then went with him to apologize to the neighbor and agree to fix the fence. Sharon reported that Terrance learned something important from that experience.

Interestingly enough, Jules's dad had a completely different response. He excused his son's behavior to the police officer as "boys will be boys," and yelled at his son for embarrassing him with the neighbors. Which boy do you think gained the most from that experience? The way parents respond to life's challenges can mean all the difference between a child's growth in conscience development and weakening it.

Most children make an important developmental shift from doing what's right to avoid a consequence to doing what's right because it's the right thing to do. Avoiding something just for the sake of consequences is a weak form of moral motivation. It's external. The best kind of motivation takes place on the inside when a child does what's right because he has the internal character to stay true to values. Look for ways to affirm internal motivation while at the same time implementing the consequences as necessary.

The Complexity of Living a Moral Life in Today's World

Children face myriad challenges when they're at school, in the neighborhood, and over at a friend's house. In each situation, they see others who are living in a way that communicates a philosophy of life. Teachers, friends, and other leaders often do and say things that are contrary to what you believe to be right and true. That's why it's so important to teach your children why you do what you do. Children need to know and understand the truth about the Christian life. A biblical worldview helps children integrate their faith into life and face the challenges they experience every day. Many of those challenges are subtle attacks on their personal faith.

One mom decided she wanted her children to attend public school so she could help them face the opposing worldview they might encounter. She says, "I want to help my children get a Christian education by attending a public school." Mom regularly equips her kids to take a stand for righteousness and to share their faith, and she helps them process the situations in which they find themselves. She also teaches her children how to accept differences in what others believe without allowing those differences to conform their thinking.

The Bible verse that became a motto in her home is Romans 12:2: "Do not conform any longer to the pattern of this world, but be transformed by the renewing of your mind. Then you will be able to test and approve what God's will is—his good, pleasing and perfect will." As each new situation arises, her children learn to "test" their response and see if it pleases God and conforms to his will.

Each family is different, and when to protect your child in order to nurture his faith or when to help him grow under pressure is a decision requiring wisdom and prayer. Parents become the tour guides on the path of life, helping their children process what they're experiencing and seeing. All kids find themselves with others and are exposed to people who don't share the same values and convictions. Your work to prepare your child and then process his or her experiences helps further strengthen that child's conscience.

> Parents become the tour guides on the path of life, helping their children process what they're experiencing and seeing.

When children recognize the value of the conscience in their lives, they're more apt to respond to its promptings. At times, it acts like a warning device, providing indicators of trouble ahead. Other times it prompts a person to take action, be responsible, or care for someone else. The warning lights flash when dishonesty is present. When children learn to pick up on the cues of the conscience, they become more responsible and more effective in life.

Teaching About the Conscience

One of the ways to help kids do what's right is to talk about the inner motivations they experience. One dad said it this way: "I tell my kids that when they feel uncomfortable about something, it's important to ask why. Usually when you feel uncomfortable, it's because something important is going on inside your heart. If God is speaking to you or your conscience is making you feel uncomfortable, try to figure out the best way to respond. It's not easy sometimes, but don't let your desire to fit in or your fear of embarrassment keep you from doing what's right. Think about it, and try to figure out what to do. If you get stuck, try to explain the situation to someone else and see if you can get some advice. Your uncomfortable feeling is likely an indication of an opportunity to do what's right and a test of your moral character, so don't miss out on the opportunity."

The family is a laboratory for growth. Kids and parents test out various ideas in the lab and develop a greater commitment to follow the Lord in all they do. It's not good enough just to find out what works, because sometimes what works isn't right for kids or for parents.

For example, when parents yell at kids, it works. Children stop being wild, get in the car, or work on their chores. But the fact that it seems to work doesn't make it right. When parents use anger as a motivator, children don't learn to do what's right. Rather, they learn to be people pleasers, looking to avoid the next parental explosion.

God designed the conscience to help guide the heart in the right direction. But the conscience is incomplete without the spiritual leadership of the Holy Spirit inside. Faith development in children is strategic for building moral thinking and for recognizing that the internal promptings they experience fit into a bigger picture of God's work in the world and in people's hearts. The second half of this book will help you know how to encourage and stimulate spiritual development in your kids. As you tie spiritual growth and conscience development together for your kids, they'll develop the internal guidance system for the heart in accordance with God's design.

As you help your child strengthen the conscience and contribute to moral development, you're passing on a valuable gift that your child will use forever. There's no sweeter peace than a heart that is sensitive to God's leadership and direction.

PART 2

Spiritual Development in Children

11

God's Plan

If parents have an unnoticeable faith, that's
the faith they're passing on to their kids.

M y son is four years old, and he's failing preschool." Sheila
sat in my (Scott's) office because the preschool her son
attended told her she needed help.

"What do you mean? What's the problem?"

"Well, they didn't actually say he's failing, but that's how I
feel. They say he cries a lot when he's there, and he doesn't join
in with the other kids in their activities."

"Maybe he's not ready for preschool yet. You aren't working
outside the home. Why do you send him to preschool?"

"I picked that school because they are Christians. I want my
son to learn about the Bible."

"Really? Did you know that you're the best person to teach
your son about the Bible?"

"I don't really know that much about the Bible."

"What a great time to learn. You and your son can learn
together about God's Word. You could read the stories in the
Bible and then apply them to both of your lives. We're not

opposed to preschool in general, but it certainly isn't best for every child."

Something happened that day in Sheila's heart. She bought a children's Bible and took on the primary responsibility for teaching her son about God and his Word.

Some parents feel inadequate to pass the faith on to their children because they don't have enough Bible knowledge or don't have strong teaching skills. Maybe that's why so many parents delegate the job of spiritual nurturing to the church or to a Christian school. But Deuteronomy only gives one prerequisite to passing the faith on to your kids: that you have an active, growing faith yourself. In speaking to parents, God says in Deuteronomy 6:6, "These commandments that I give you today are to be upon *your* hearts." Notice what it doesn't say. You don't have to be enrolled in a Bible college or seminary to do the job. All you need is a real faith. You want to have the commands of God on and in your heart.

> A complete understanding of internal motivation in children must involve the work of God in that child's life.

A complete understanding of internal motivation in children must involve the work of God in that child's life. Internal motivation comes from the heart, but the heart provides promptings from several places all at the same time. Children need help sorting out and managing things like desires, emotions, and the conscience. The Holy Spirit is God and comes to live inside the heart to first transform it by his grace and then to be the personal counselor, teacher, helper, and even a source of power to face life's challenges.

It's true that other things may seem more urgent, but when all is said and done, there's nothing more crucial to a child's success than having a strong personal faith. Not only does that faith assure you that you'll spend eternity together in heaven, but it also dramatically contributes to a child's well-being between now and then.

Level three thinking involves considering how faith applies to life, how to respond well to conscience promptings, and ways to listen to the Holy Spirit in daily life. Kids then learn to be responsible and grow in their maturity. God calls everyone to live on a different level when he says in Colossians 3:2, "Set your minds on things above, not on earthly things." Romans 8:5 says, "Those who live according to the sinful nature have their minds set on what that nature desires; but those who live in accordance with the Spirit have their minds set on what the Spirit desires." As children become more conscious of the Holy Spirit and the conscience in their lives, they learn to live on a different level, one that considers what God wants for them, not just their own desires.

Too many children today are raised on simple behavior modification. That approach to life trains children to think about themselves and overemphasizes level one thinking. When parents help their children practice faith, rely on the Holy Spirit, and pay attention to the promptings of the conscience, they're contributing to the long-term maturity and health of their kids. It often requires that parents retrain themselves to relate to their kids in more strategic ways, but the work pays off with huge dividends.

Kids were placed in a family to learn about God, his Word, and his plan for their lives. When they catch hold of the spiritual dimension of life, amazing things happen inside their hearts. Can children think on a third level? Yes, they can, and living in a family is the place where God designed that thinking to develop.

In the Old Testament, we read how God prepared the Israelite families for entering into a new stage of their lives. It's surprising how similar the believers in Moses' day are to us in the twenty-first century. Let's look at the story.

In the book of Deuteronomy, the believers were preparing to possess the land of Canaan. Over the last several years, they'd learned to trust the Lord in their own lives as they wandered in the wilderness. Now they wanted to move forward to obey God and serve him. Deuteronomy contains the story of the rededication of their lives and the instructions God gave for how to go forward with him, both personally and in their families.

These believers were headed into a new land where a number of evil influences threatened their spiritual health. Huge temptations loomed for their children. The people who currently lived in the land had practices that went against God's values. How would the Israelites be successful in a world that was so pagan? These people were just like us. They loved God, loved their kids, wanted to serve the Lord, and wanted to raise families committed to him, and they would need to do that while living in a land of evil influences and temptations that could rob them of God's blessings.

It's interesting to note that in the previous forty years, all the men of fighting age had died in the wilderness. That was part of God's judgment on the people for being unwilling to obey his leadership. Likely, there were a number of single parents and blended families among the Israelite nation. Even so, the instructions Moses gave to the people applied to every form of family out there, not just to traditional families. The instructions were for moms, dads, grandparents, adoptive parents, and anyone caring for kids.

As the Old Testament story unfolds, the Israelites go forward and do great things for God. But many would also fail. Some children would marry pagan wives. Sin was waiting at every turn. What would make these believers successful as they found themselves living in a world full of pitfalls on all sides? The answer is found in Moses' instructions to them in Deuteronomy 6. He started by telling the parents what they must do. Verse 6 says, "These commandments that I give you today are to be upon your hearts."

Discipleship in the family starts with the parents' commitment to God's commands. Raising children is the most challenging experience you'll probably ever have. Your commitment to the Lord will help you get through the tough times and know how to help your child through many challenges of life. The Bible contains the wisdom you'll need to teach your kids how to deal with sibling conflict, how to accept no for an answer, and how to respond well to correction. God provides tools and methodology, and the more you study God's Word, the easier it will be for your children to receive the faith that has empowered you.

> Discipleship in the family starts with the parents' commitment to God's commands.

Verses 7–9 continue by giving specific instructions for parents: "Impress them on your children. Talk about them when you sit at home and when you walk along the road, when you lie down and when you get up. Tie them as symbols on your hands and bind them on your foreheads. Write them on the doorframes of your houses and on your gates."

Three Principles

You can break Moses' instructions into three principles:

1. Build relationship.
2. Share Scripture.
3. Practice faith.

These three principles form the basis for the "how to" presented in these next few chapters. As you apply these three principles to passing on the faith to your children, you'll maximize your kids' interaction with God and his Word.

You *build relationship* by being with your kids when they sit at home, travel with you in the van, snuggle with you at bedtime, and eat breakfast with you in the morning. Building relationship provides the vehicle through which values pass from one generation to the next. But building relationship with your kids is not enough.

You also need to *share Scripture*. Moses said that parents are to impress God's commands upon their children. Sharing Scripture with kids helps them see that the Bible is relevant, practical, and exciting. God's commands are the standard by which we live. We are all accountable to God for our lives.

Practicing faith actually shows children how to apply the Scriptures to their lives. The Deuteronomy passage talks about tying them as symbols on your hands and binding them on your foreheads. Those are practi-

God is concerned
about the
details of life.

cal ways to keep the Scriptures in front of you. When you make the Bible accessible for kids, they learn in practical ways what it means to demonstrate faith, hope, and love. Actions such as prayer, Bible study, service, compassion, money management, and commitment to God's church come out of the commands of God. Children pick up their faith from their parents, whatever that faith is.

Kids learn from their parents how to handle unfairness, manage resources, and think about others. If you're connected to God and his Word, your kids will see what it means to serve God in practical ways. Children are learning a biblical world-view as they live in a home where parents are seeking to serve the

Lord. No greater gift can equip your children to be successful.

Level three thinking is simply the conscious realization that God is always at work, that he often reveals himself and his activity to us in numerous ways, and that we are a part of his plan. God is concerned about the details of life. If there's any question, just look at how Psalm 139 describes God's intimate knowledge of our personal lives:

> You know when I sit and when I rise; you perceive my thoughts from afar. You discern my going out and my lying down; you are familiar with all my ways. Before a word is on my tongue you, LORD, know it completely. You hem me in—behind and before; you have laid your hand upon me. Such knowledge is too wonderful for me, too lofty for me to attain. (vv. 2–6)

God isn't distant. He's personal. He cares for each person in a special and unique way. Even the child who has not yet made a commitment to Jesus is the recipient of God's grace and love. When kids live with that reality, it makes a dramatic impact on their hearts.

But My Church Trains
My Kids Spiritually

Some might ask a good question, "Since I don't feel adequate to pass the faith on to my kids, why don't I just have the professionals do it at church or in the Christian school?" That's a great question, and misunderstanding its answer has resulted in many children leaving the faith as they grow into adulthood. The church does have an important role here. It's twofold: to equip parents to be spiritual trainers and to complement what parents are doing at home.

However, when parents give up the job and allow the church to do it instead, children miss out on the most important dimension of passing on the faith to the next generation: seeing that faith is relevant in daily life. Passing on the faith is more than imparting biblical knowledge or explaining theology. It's living it out. When children see faith lived out in the everyday activities of life, they're more apt to catch it. If they're just gaining head knowledge or simply engaged in wholesome activities at church, without seeing it practiced at home, they tend to see the Bible and church as irrelevant to day-to-day life. Many of these children then "grow out of" their parents' faith as they get older.

> Passing on the faith is more than imparting biblical knowledge or explaining theology.

The church, like the family, is designed to be a discipleship center, building into the lives of people. But sometimes the church, in its eagerness to meet all people at their points of need, goes a bit too far, taking on some of the responsibilities of the family. Instead of encouraging parents to step up and take on their role of spiritual trainers, the church sometimes says, "We'll take care of this spiritual training of children. Just leave it to us." When that happens, some parents give up their God-given responsibility of passing the faith on to their kids.

Or, to be fair to the church, sometimes the family just isn't doing its job, so the church steps in and teaches the Bible to kids in real and exciting ways. The church does have a responsibility to train and disciple every person, both young and old, so teaching kids the Bible and helping them understand the faith does fit under the church's job description. However, without the parent-training link, kids miss out on something very significant. Parents sometimes don't realize this and believe that delegating the work of spiritual training to the church fulfills their job.

It's not a matter of one or the other. Both are important. Church programs are a good tool for enhancing children's spiritual development, but without the parents being spiritual trainers at home, kids miss out on the core of what it means to be godly. The result is that some children grow out of faith or somehow view faith as something that happens at church but isn't integrated into their whole lives. In the end, kids receive Bible knowledge, and they even make spiritual commitments, but the full integration of their faith is often lacking. The key is, parents must take on their role as primary spiritual trainers so their kids catch the faith they are trying to pass on to them.

Prepared to Face the Challenges of Life

As the Deuteronomy believers faced the challenge of conquering the promised land, they and their children encountered a number of obstacles. One was living in an environment that had ungodly influences all around. Deuteronomy 7 describes the nations that lived in that land. Their ungodliness created temptations that would be hard for the new inhabitants to withstand. God wanted his people to be successful in the midst of all the challenges they would face. That's why he gave the instructions in Deuteronomy 6 mentioned earlier. It's the same today. When parents are active in their faith, transparent in their spiritual growth, and eager to pass on the faith to their kids, those children are better equipped to face the challenges all around them.

Your kids are bombarded by worldly influences. How will they think about living their lives as chosen people entering a promised land full of blessings? Staying true to God and his instructions will protect them from myriad temptations and pitfalls. It's great to provide your kids with spiritual activities and a good church where they can learn and grow, but nothing can replace the impact of your role as spiritual discipler of your children. It's powerful. It's God's design.

The Benefits of Grandparents

First, let's talk about the benefits grandparents bring to a family, and then we'll look at some of the challenges. Biblically, there's no doubt that the role of grandparent is an important one. Psalm 78 gives a beautiful statement about the legacy grandparents pass on. Verses 3–4 talk about "what we have heard and known, what our fathers have told us. We will not hide them from their children." The passage continues, "We will tell the next generation the praiseworthy deeds of the LORD, his power, and the wonders he has done."

Grandparents serve many roles, often emphasizing some of these more than others. They may be the family historians, wise confidants, playmates, babysitters, mentors, and tradition keepers, passing on memorable experiences to their children and grandchildren. In some families, grandparents have become the primary caretakers, managing the day-to-day work of family life and raising the children.

Some grandparents may not be able to solve the Internet problems or know how to play a video game, but they do know a thing or two about life, love, hope, sorrow, disappointment, success, failure, and God's love. Some are able to provide assistance in a family by contributing financially, giving emotional support, helping with homework, and assisting with child care. At the same time, grandchildren bring laughter, energy, perspective, love, and gratefulness to the hearts of grandparents.

Christian grandparents have a spiritual heritage that's worth repeating. Even those who have recently become Christians can pass on spiritual history of the faith to their grandkids. Many grandparents have more time and may be more relaxed about life than their children, and thus are better able to create comfortable relationships. They sometimes aren't as involved in the day-to-day busyness of family life, allowing them to focus more on relationship development. Furthermore, because grandparents are often not as engaged in the daily correction or discipline of the children, they can focus more on nurture, taking opportunities to give children perspective on life and to support the parents in their child training.

Christian grandparents have a spiritual heritage that's worth repeating.

The only time the word *grandmother* is used in the Bible is in 2 Timothy 1:5: "I have been reminded of your sincere faith, which first lived in your grandmother Lois and in your mother Eunice and, I am persuaded, now lives in you also." An interesting word occurs in this verse to describe the faith that Timothy had. It's the word *sincere* and literally means "not hypocritical." Children and grandchildren long to see a faith that is real in the lives of others. It's one thing to take kids to church. It's another to allow them to see a genuine integrity in your faith at home. That's the message that Timothy learned from the influence of his mother and grandmother. Timothy caught it, and children can catch it today, too, when they see it lived out in the everyday life of others, especially those in the family.

The Family Challenge

Our goal in this section of the book is to lay out for you a practical plan to pass the faith on to your kids. We call it the Family Challenge. When you take the Family Challenge and commit to build relationship, share Scripture, and practice faith at least one structured time each week, great things will happen in you and your kids. Spontaneous conversations about God, his Word, and faith then spring up in the course of life. As you view your family as a mission field or a ministry opportunity, God will provide opportunities for you. And your family itself will grow closer together. Your children will have a continual flow of godly thinking into their lives that can impact their hearts in strategic ways and change their internal motivations for the better. The next few chapters will show you how to make it happen in your family in practical ways.

12

Family Time
Once a Week

Take your kids to church – 10 points.
Worship at church with them – 25 points.
Serve Christ with your kids – 50 points.
Teach your kids the Bible at home – 100 points.

Techniques for passing the faith on to kids look different from one home to the next. Furthermore, one child may need an approach that's different from the one used with another child, even if they're both in the same family. Biblical insights and practical discussions happen at all kinds of times and in many different places. Although informal opportunities for connecting take place in most families, kids also benefit from structured times of training as well. If you can make a habit of setting aside twenty to thirty minutes a week as a planned spiritual event in your family, it can lead to many informal conversations that happen spontaneously.

In this chapter, we want to share with you an idea that works. We call it Family Time, and it's a great way to practically take the Family Challenge in your home. By having a planned Family Time, your kids will grow to expect your spiritual leadership and develop the godly character that's an outgrowth of spiritual training.

An Inside Look

To illustrate what this looks like, we want to tell you about three families. The Martinez family has a dad, mom, and three children, ages four, seven, and nine. The second family is made up of Shirley Swanson, a single mom, and her two teenage daughters, ages fourteen and sixteen. The third family is the Jones/Cordova family, a blended family with a sixteen- and a nineteen-year-old of Dad's from a previous marriage, and a three- and a five-year-old that Dad and Mom have together. All three families are committed to Christ and eager to pass the faith on to their kids. They all have regular Family Times. Here are their stories.

> Then comes the question that the kids have learned to expect: "What's the lesson learned?"

Three years ago, Peter and Ann Martinez started a regular Family Time with the goal of teaching their children from God's Word. It was a big hit from the very beginning. Family Time is regularly announced with their family theme song, and the whole family comes to eat together. They typically have paper plates and something simple, such as pizza or tacos. The conversation around the table is fun as they talk about their day, tell stories, and laugh together. Everyone loves Family Time.

After dinner the kids wait in anticipation as Dad or Mom reads the Bible passage to set the stage for the activity. Sometimes it's a story about Jesus or one of the great heroes from the Bible. Other times it's a verse or two from a New Testament epistle.

Then comes the question the kids have learned to expect: "What's the lesson learned?" Kids and parents suggest applications of the verses for their daily lives.

Next, there is an activity that is typically the highlight. Usually it means running around in some form of high-energy experience. One time they had a race with baggy clothes on to illustrate Hebrews 12:1: "Therefore, since we are surrounded by such a great cloud of witnesses, let us throw off everything that hinders and the sin that so easily entangles, and let us run with perseverance the race marked out for us." Another time they poked a hole in a can of soda and shot it all over the fence, illustrating the mess that anger makes when you don't keep it under control as stated in Proverbs 29:11: "A fool gives full vent to his anger, but a wise man keeps himself under control." Yet another time they turned off all the lights in the house and tried to follow a treasure map, running around the house with flashlights to illustrate Psalm 119:105: "Your word is a lamp to my feet and a light for my path."

After the activity, they gathered together as a family to debrief about what they'd learned and to talk again about how they might apply the Bible to their lives. Lastly, they prayed together, allowing each person in the family to share a few words with the Lord.

Family Time will always be remembered at the Martinez home. It's part of their legacy. Children often refer back to the fun times they've shared and enjoy telling about their favorite Family Times. Occasionally they invite friends to join in the fun. The children are all young, and it's clear that they're learning what faith looks like in practical terms.

The Swanson family is quite different. Unfortunately, Shirley Swanson and her husband divorced about five years ago. Since that time, Shirley has committed herself to raising her teenage daughters, Nicole and Jeannie, in a way that puts Christ at the center of their family. They've been doing Family Time at least once a week, but the schedule is rarely the same. They're all very busy, so often their time together is on Saturday evenings, but sometimes it's on a weekday evening. Mom keeps the calendar and is often asking, "If we do all these things, when will we have our Family Time?"

On the evening of Family Time, they eat together and then clean up the kitchen. Sometimes they talk about the Bible over the meal, and other times they gather in the living room for a discussion. The leadership of Family Time rotates among each of them. Mom started that two years ago, and it always keeps things interesting. They often study a book of the Bible, each taking a chapter at a time to read, explain, and illustrate with some form of activity. The planning is part of the fun, as each person has to ask the question, "How could we illustrate this truth in a fun way?" Occasionally the leader can't think of an activity, so they brainstorm together and develop one on the fly.

One time, when it was Nicole's turn to lead, they were studying the book of James and came to the end of chapter 2, where it talks about faith without works being dead. Nicole decided to make some cookies the next afternoon, and after dinner they delivered them to three neighbors, just to encourage them. It was a simple activity, but meaningful nonetheless.

Another time, when they were studying the gospel of Matthew, Mom had them each create their own parable to illustrate some kind of truth about God. They all laughed together as Jeannie started her parable, "Once upon a time, there was a mom who had two daughters . . ." The prayer times on this evening were especially meaningful as they prayed for one another and the challenges they were each facing. Mom says, "Our schedules keep us on the run. We don't even get to eat together many of our days, but Family Time keeps our relationships close."

Bill Jones and Haley Cordova have a problem that required a bit of creativity to overcome in order for them to enjoy Family Time together. Bill's older kids are with them every other week, and there's a significant age difference between them and the younger kids. It seemed as if any Family Time with the younger kids would leave out the older ones.

So that every child could participate in Family Time, many times the parents would hold two different Family Times. That seemed to work well, but occasionally they would focus on the younger ones and have a Family Time as if with four adults, rather than two, and the two young children. The partnering together of the four older people to work with the younger kids accomplished their goal of fostering closeness as a family, teaching truths from the Bible, and everyone learning in the process. On one evening, they had piggyback races to illustrate Galatians 6:2, which says, "Carry each other's burdens, and in this way you will fulfill the law of Christ." Then they talked about how they can support each other during the day. Even the younger kids could do things to help out.

> "We don't even get to eat together many of our days, but Family Time keeps our relationships close."

Another time they talked about the value of childlike faith from Matthew 18:2–4: "He called a little child and had him stand among them. And he said: 'I tell you the truth, unless you change and become like little children, you will never enter the kingdom of heaven. Therefore, whoever humbles himself like this child is the greatest in the kingdom of heaven.'" They allowed the younger kids to lead the blindfolded teens around a maze. The young people in this family learned about spiritual leadership as they watched their parents look for ways to teach God's Word. It became a valuable teaching time for all.

Making Family Time Work in Your Family

These three families are all unique, but they have one thing in common: a commitment to sharing God's Word as a family. Parents in each family are committed to passing the faith on to their children. The Family Times in each home looked different, but they all shared common ingredients. What might Family Time look like in your home? As you consider developing a Family Time, here are some things that will make it work.

1. *Schedule it.* Although it may not be the same time every week, put it on the calendar. Even if you don't have something specific planned yet, putting it on the schedule can help keep it a priority in family life. As we all know, the calendar can get filled up quite quickly. Your work in the scheduling department is the first step of commitment your family needs to make Family Time happen.

   The family schedule is one of those areas where balance is essential. When family members get overcommitted, the family experiences pressure. You might get all the items done in a week, but that's not the goal. The goal is to equip children for the future. A schedule is one of the ways to keep a family balanced. When the family gets off balance, the kids begin to miss out on what's most important.

2. *Ask, "What's the lesson learned?"* After reading a Bible passage, it's important to apply its underlying principle to life. It's fun to watch kids take the Bible to heart. In one

family, they talked about confessing faults after reading James 5:16, "Confess your sins to each other and pray for each other so that you may be healed." Mom admitted that she was working on her anger when she got frustrated in family life. Her daughter then admitted that she was working on obedience without complaining, something they had talked about the previous day. Mom was impressed that her daughter was willing to share such an important thing she was working on. Furthermore, now it could be an item of prayer, and they could partner together on a new level.

> The Family Times in each home looked different, but they all shared common ingredients.

By asking the question, "What's the lesson learned?" at every Family Time, children recognize that the Bible is practical and that it's the authority for life. Kids see how the Bible is relevant for their lives. Integrating the Bible into life is strategic for helping children develop level three thinking. Furthermore, the principles of God's Word provide a standard for the conscience to rely on, and kids develop convictions about life. In short, a new form of internal motivation grows and develops in your child's heart.

3. *Do an activity.* Often an activity has the ability to get through to a child in a way that a discussion can't. If you can't think of an activity in advance, ask your family for an activity idea during the Family Time itself. Kids tend to be creative, and the brainstorming you do may stimulate an idea that's just perfect. Furthermore, thinking about the activity together helps kids examine the faith principle more carefully as they try to come up with an idea to illustrate it.

Activities come in many forms. You might think about a game, contest, or race. Or maybe you could do a service project or reach out beyond the walls of your home by writing, calling, visiting, or caring for others. Drama, art, and music are also fun ways to illustrate God's Word. Science, cooking, and experiments are intriguing as well.

In fact, you might think of a fun or creative activity first and then work backward and look for a Bible passage or story that it might illustrate. That's what Kathy did when she saw how a drop of soap on the surface of water pushed flakes of pepper to the side. She knew her kids would enjoy the activity, so she tried to think of a biblical truth it might illustrate. She landed on the idea of gentleness with others. They discussed what gentleness means in practical terms, and then she shared the Bible verse for the evening, Proverbs 15:1: "A gentle answer turns away wrath, but a harsh word stirs up anger." The discussion continued throughout the week, providing ways to practice gentleness to repel conflict.

> As you get into the routine of Family Time in your home, you'll see children change and your family grow closer together.

The National Center for Biblical Parenting has a series of books called Family Time Activities. These books, written by Kirk Weaver, are excellent tools for the spiritual training of your children in fun ways.

The reason Family Times work to pass the faith on to kids is because they are encouraging all three things taught in Deuteronomy 6:7–9: building relationship, sharing Scripture, and practicing faith. As you tie all those together strategically in twenty to thirty minutes a week, an amazing thing happens to your children. They begin to see what faith in God is all about and even begin to feel some things about God that they may not have realized otherwise. It's encouraging and even fun for parents to hear their kids discussing lessons they've learned and applying them at other times during the week.

As you get into the routine of Family Time in your home, you'll see children change and your family grow closer together. Most important, you'll be passing the faith on to your kids in ways that they can understand and apply to their hearts and lives. In the next chapters we'll go more in depth about the three ingredients that make passing the faith on to your kids work best.

13

Relationship Is Foundational

Family is the most influential human relationship in a person's life, whether you want it to be or not.

J enny shared her story with determination and a hint of disappointment. "As I was growing up, I didn't have a very close relationship with my mom. I felt like she didn't like me. I wanted my relationship with my daughter to be different. I've gone out of my way to make our home a safe place for her to talk and share. I take a personal interest in her life. But now that she's thirteen, it seems to be harder. She doesn't share the same things with me as she did before. I need new strategies to connect with my daughter."

Unfortunately, some parents, unlike Jenny, are content to allow the teen years to create a chasm in the personal relationship between parent and child. Some believe it just has to be that way. Others seem too tired to do the work to build new bridges. When parents change the way they interact with their teens, even closer relationships are possible. Deeper conversations, significant interactions, and positive experiences can make the teen years a rewarding time for both the young person and the parent. Spiritual interaction is strategic and requires a bit more forethought than in the earlier years. Whether your child is younger or older, you'll want to take advantage of

> Relationship is more than just living together as a family.

the three strategies from Deuteronomy 6: *build relationship*, *share Scripture*, and *practice faith*. In this chapter, we'll discuss the first strategy of building relationship, since that's the channel through which the other two components become effective. Building relationship is foundational to passing the faith on to your kids.

So what is relationship, how do we build it, and why is it important? Relationship is more than just living together as a family. Relationship implies a deeper connection. It's a heart response toward one another that says, "I know you; I like you; I enjoy being with you." When parents and children have a strong relationship, they value one another and are open to learn.

Building relationship comes naturally for some parents but is more difficult for others. Nonetheless, it's not optional. Close relationships between parents and children are the tool to help kids catch the convictions they'll need to be the world-changers God intends for them to be.

Let's Get Practical

So how do you do it? Relationships don't just happen, and certainly maintaining close relationships takes work. Some parents find connecting with young children easy. They curl up on the couch for a special read-aloud or a favorite movie. The shared experience leads to gentle hugs and feelings of closeness. Tickling games, fun desserts, cute nicknames, and family outings all bring closeness to families with young children.

Older children often connect with their parents differently than when they were younger. Conversations about feelings and opinions, playing games together, and sharing in a hobby or skill help parents and teens connect in heartfelt ways. Here are a few things to keep in mind when seeking to build relationship.

1. *Be intentional.* If you're expecting relationship to grow on its own, you may be disappointed. Take initiative to get to know your child's heart. Try different things and make mental notes about what works and what doesn't.

2. *Stay focused.* If the goal of an activity is to deepen closeness, then save the instruction giving and correction session for another time. Noncritical listening breeds closeness. Eye contact and physical touch say, "I'm interested in you." Parents should always be sensitive to the relational component of their parenting, but some events and activities can have the primary goal of developing closeness. In that case, you may choose to postpone correction times that may work against your goal.

   For this few minutes, you may have to look past the wiggles of a preschooler or the misplaced values of a preteen. You'll likely come back to those issues later, but in this particular moment, stay focused on relationship as much as you can. Of course, that's not always possible. Sometimes parenting requires that you give up what you thought might be a special relational time because a child needs some form of discipline now. Hopefully, though, there are times when you're able to focus on building relationship as the goal.

3. *Be available.* Relationships don't always grow on a schedule. Your elementary-age child may open her heart to you just as you're trying to tuck her in at night. Your teenager may come home from an activity and be eager to talk. Be on the lookout for opportunities when your child is reaching out to you. It may be subtle or at a "bad" time, but if possible, stop what you're doing and give your full attention.

4. *Activities help.* Working together to accomplish a goal is a great relationship-building tool. Cleaning the garage, making a new recipe for dinner, or going on a family trip to the park all have the potential to deepen relationship. Working and playing together build connection.

5. *Develop traditions.* Family traditions bring closeness and develop strong family bonds. Holiday traditions, vacation traditions, or even Saturday morning breakfast traditions all contribute to relationship building.

6. *Watch your timing and listen.* Sometimes older children respond well to being treated like adults. Sometimes they need to relive tender moments in more playful ways. Building relationship requires careful observation and sensitivity in order to meet kids where they are and connect in ways that touch their hearts.

Keep the Goal in Mind

Remember, however, that building relationship is not an end in and of itself. Some parents miss this truth and end up with a family that's self-focused. God has given the family a bigger purpose to embrace. A strong family seeks to bless others, cares for others, and helps them find God in tangible ways.

In short, the family is a place where children become

disciples of Jesus Christ so they can impact the world. They learn how to become disciple-makers themselves. Some parents miss these essential goals, believing instead that they're simply trying to raise mature, responsible kids. Yet God designed the family to be a disciple-making center, where children learn what it means to serve the Lord and then reach out and help others see what a life committed to God is all about. That family can be a strategic vehicle for transforming the world. Children learn how to hold convictions, solve problems, and communicate a biblical worldview in a way that advances God's kingdom in the home, neighborhood, school, and the world.

> A strong family seeks to bless others, cares for others, and helps them find God in tangible ways.

Biblical principles are taught in the home in everyday experiences such as handling conflict, working on chores, and getting ready in the morning. Close relationships between parents and children are important because they mimic the kind of love God has for his children. Relationship is foundational, and God uses his relationship with us to help us learn and grow. In the same way, your relationship with your children is a springboard for helping them catch the faith and live it out on a daily basis.

Relationship is more than just spending time together. It involves connecting with a child's heart. Some parents think that when family jobs are complete, they can enjoy some much-needed rest, but typically additional times of relationship building are necessary to develop strong family bonds. One very committed mom who homeschooled her kids said, "I used to think I was earning all the relationship points I needed by homeschooling my kids each day, but then I realized that my children needed more from me. I needed to spend time with them enjoying relationship and having fun outside of school time in order to experience closeness with my kids. It seems that the teaching often puts a drain on our relationship that I need to balance out in other ways."

The foundation of parenting is relationship, not family business. Before parents enter into the business of parenting, they're in relationship with their children. Relationship comes before duty. It's true that parents must engage in the business of parenting by giving instructions, correcting, and setting limits. Those are very important parts of a parent's job description. Keep in mind, though, that those things often put pressure on the relationship. Therefore, it's important to intentionally work on building relationship with each of your children. Since being a parent can quickly focus on tasks, it's important that parents seek ways to connect emotionally even in the midst of the jobs of family life. It's when the relational connectedness between family members decreases significantly that tension increases, and a parent's ability to teach and influence decreases as well.

> The foundation of parenting is relationship, not family business.

Two Things to Remember

Two parenting strategies help increase the closeness among family members. Both take time. Each approaches the challenge in different ways. The first is *initiative*, and the second is *responsiveness*. Both require margin or extra time in the schedule and flexibility in one's personal agenda.

Initiative looks for ways to consider the other person's interests, needs, and desires. What is your child's favorite food, color, friend, or activity? What are the top three stressors in your teen's life? What longings, hopes, and desires does your child have? When you know the answers to these kinds of questions, you can initiate in meaningful ways. Children see that you care when you take interest in the details and passions of their lives. It might be by making their favorite cookies or bringing home an idea from work that delights your child. You see your daughter's eyes light up, and you know that you've touched her heart. You might ask yourself, "What can I do to bring joy into my child's life?" It's not about giving things to a child; it's about knowing your child's heart and demonstrating that you care.

Because each child is unique and different, it's easier to connect with some kids than with others. Some children are external processors, so you know everything they're thinking, providing easy opportunities to identify interests in common and areas to pursue. Internal processors may be more of a puzzle to their parents and might need different ways to experience closeness with Mom or Dad.

Remember that the daily work of family life typically results in a slow drain on relationship. Getting the house cleaned up, kids ready in the morning, and homework done, and taxiing kids from one location to another can be a challenge for any manager. The work involved to get food on the table and clothes cleaned and back in drawers is stressful and has the potential to put pressure on family dynamics. Initiating relationship regularly is like adding oil to the machine to reduce friction so tasks are easier to accomplish.

Initiative is proactive. Responsiveness, on the other hand, puts you in observation mode, always on the lookout for an opportunity to connect. Responsiveness keeps a ready attitude for those moments when your child expresses a need to talk. The child who is overwhelmed with excitement about a new opportunity or is discouraged by a disappointing event both have one thing in common—an opportunity for a parent to connect on a heart level. Although advice and problem-solving may help in those moments, it's most important to share the emotion and empathize with your child's feelings. When you do, you can connect with your child's heart.

Initiative reminds you to think about your child. Responsiveness keeps you ready for the surprises that may come along at any time. Both help contribute to relationship building, and if you take advantage of the opportunities, you may have some significant relational connections.

Relationship Heightens
Spiritual Sensitivity

Opportunities for closeness regularly present themselves, but recognizing them is only part of the challenge. The other part is bringing faith into life in practical ways. That doesn't mean that every emotional experience needs a Bible verse or a prayer time. That would seem artificial, especially as your children get older. But spiritual sensitivity often increases when emotions are involved. Parents can help frame the picture for their children by moving excitement to gratefulness for God's provision or discouragement to relying on God's grace. Spirituality, in part, is a way of thinking, and often parents can help children integrate their faith into what might otherwise appear to be mundane, everyday tasks. In short, relationship provides the conduit through which parents mold the most intricate parts of a child's heart. Kids pick up new ways to think, truths to believe, and ultimately an internal motivation that's pleasing to God.

Deuteronomy 6:7–9 suggests four opportunities for relationship building: when you sit at home, when you walk along the road, when you lie down, and when you get up. In reality, this passage was talking about all aspects of life together, but translated into modern times, we can interpret it to mean when you're hanging out at home, traveling somewhere, going through your morning routine, or preparing for bed. Those are four strategic times that provide relationship opportunities.

One mom affirmed the benefit of traveling together by saying, "When we're in the van, I have a captive audience. I try to plan stimulating questions or stories to get the kids talking and interacting. We require some of our van time to be without electronics. Video games are shut down, headphones get put away, and the radio is off. It usually takes a bit of recovery time for kids to reenter a relational mode. They don't often bounce right into conversation, having been fully engaged in an electronic battle with the universe. In fact, sometimes they even resent having to leave their electronic friends. I know that it takes a bit of time to disengage with electronics and start connecting relationally, so I'm patient to allow that to happen. Typically, after a few minutes, a lively conversation erupts. Sometimes we share about our day, and other times we talk about something that's happening, or share opinions about an idea."

Storytelling about life and reminiscing about past common experiences are good ways to draw children into the conversation. When you make these practices common, children learn to create their own conversation, tell their own stories, and ask their own questions. Listening and responding to your children increase openness.

One parent shared this observation: "I longed for my daughter to learn how to drive. She's seventeen now, and she's been driving for six months. I didn't realize what I'd lose when she got her driver's license. We used to talk in the car as I drove her to sports, church, and other activities. Now she's gone a lot, driving herself to work and all her activities. I miss our times together in the car. We're having to find new ways to connect. If I had known a year ago what I know now, I probably would have valued those times together more."

Using Relationship to Interact Spiritually

Some parents are fast enough on their feet to pass the faith on to their kids spontaneously. But most parents realize an opportunity after the fact, or see one developing but don't quite know how to respond in the moment. After a little while, in that case, a parent may return to a child and say, "I like what you shared during dinner today. I just want you to know that I'm praying for you." Or, "Yesterday you were talking about that problem you're having at school, and I found a verse that might be helpful."

The impact of sharing Scripture and practicing faith is much greater when it takes place in the context of building relationship. That's why we're encouraging you to take the Family Challenge. Passing the faith on to kids takes place spontaneously throughout the day, but also requires a planned time for more structured teaching.

The "build relationship" part of the Family Challenge makes your times more meaningful, and the heart connection gives opportunity for children to connect with God. It may be a favorite meal shared or laughing together over a book of riddles. It could be an activity that engages everyone in the family or just a simple conversation that sets the stage for the time together. As you look for ways to build relationship, you're teaching children an essential value in life: that relationships are important. In fact, parents can become facilitators to help children connect with God himself. And of course, that's the goal. You have a significant role as a parent. Passing on the faith doesn't only happen by reading God's Word at the table after dinner. It takes place in the daily interactions of life through the relationships you have with your kids.

14

Scripture + Creativity = Impact

Read God's Word and it will grow in
your heart. Read God's Word with
your kids and it will grow in theirs.

S ometimes a bit of creativity can change what a child believes.
That's what happened with Dan when he was fifteen. Here's
how he recounts the story.

I really wanted to go to camp one summer. I had my heart set
on it. For a number of reasons, it didn't look like it was going
to work out for me. I was very disappointed. My dad came to
me one day and said, "Do you know what a goad is?"

"Yes, it's kind of like a sheep."

"Not a goat. A goad."

"No, I don't know what that is."

"I was thinking about your desire to go to camp, and I
was reminded of the Bible story of the goad, and I thought it
might be helpful for you."

I had been a Christian most of my life, but I'd never heard a story about a goad in the Bible before, so I was curious. My dad got his Bible and turned to Acts 26:14 and read the words of Jesus to Paul: "'Saul, Saul, why do you persecute me? It is hard for you to kick against the goads.'"

"So, what's a goad?" I asked.

"It's a sharp stick used to keep the oxen on the right path. When they start going the wrong direction when plowing, the farmer pokes them a bit to keep them in line."

"Interesting, Dad, but really, what does that have to do with me and camp?"

"Well, I was thinking that the apostle Paul was quite committed to his plan to kill all the Christians. He was emotionally invested in his desires, and God sent him several indicators like goad pricks, but he wasn't able to pay attention to them, so God had to create a crisis in his life by making him blind so he could see that he was going in the wrong direction. I was thinking about your desire to go to camp and how that doesn't seem to be working out. I was just wondering if maybe you were so emotionally invested in the situation that you couldn't listen to the Lord."

That conversation with my dad had an impact on me. I started to realize that I was allowing myself to moan and groan about something I couldn't do anything about. I started to release my disappointment, and it changed my outlook. Now, as I look back on that summer, missing camp wasn't that big of a deal. Some other good things happened that summer, and I'm glad I didn't miss them. Most important, though, I learned that my disappointment could be dangerous because maybe I wouldn't be able to hear what God wanted for me.

One of the greatest benefits of the Bible is that it allows us to understand who God is, who we are, and what God's plan is for us. Communicating those things to children, though, can sometimes be quite a challenge. We must get down on their level and translate the Scriptures to each child's developmental stage. How do we do that? We follow the example of Jesus as he passed the faith on to his disciples.

> We must get down on their level and translate the Scriptures to each child's developmental stage.

Matthew 13:34 says, "Jesus spoke all these things to the crowd in parables; he did not say anything to them without using a parable." Jesus was not only concerned about what he wanted to say, but he chose carefully how he would say it to maximize the impact. I can imagine Jesus lying in bed at night saying, "I wish I could communicate to these guys that God loves each of them personally." Then, the next day, he gets up and tells his disciples a story about a shepherd who had a hundred sheep and one wanders off and gets lost. The shepherd leaves the ninety-nine and goes and gets the lost one. That's how much God loves each person.

Or maybe Jesus was trying to think about how to teach his disciples to stop judging one another. As he pondered the idea, it came to him that he'd talk about removing the plank in your own eye first before you try to get rid of the speck of sawdust in someone else's eye. It's interesting that Jesus had past experience in a carpenter's shop and may have been drawing on that experience to teach his disciples a practical kingdom principle.

As Jesus was thinking about how to teach his disciples about servanthood, he got up from the table and took a towel and washed the disciples' feet. When Jesus wanted to communicate a kingdom principle, he combined it with a story of a man walking on the road or a seed growing in the ground. We call that teaching strategy "parables." The word *parable* literally means "a casting alongside." It has the idea of bringing something alongside the truth to illustrate it or make it meaningful. The creativity helped embed the truth into the hearts of the hearers. In the same way that Jesus used stories, parents can use the language of children, which is activity, to share Scripture and communicate God's truth. Kids of any age learn through play, and what better way to help them understand the principles of Scripture than through activity?

> Kids learn through play, and what better way to help them understand the principles of Scripture than through activity?

"But I don't have a creative bone in my body," said one interested mom. That may seem true, but most people are more creative than they think, and there are many resources and tools to help parents use activity to teach children about the Bible. You'll be surprised by the creative ideas you can come up with yourself when you're studying the Scriptures and then talking to your child about them. The goal is to help kids recognize that the Bible is relevant, practical, and exciting.

The Bible Is Different from Other Books

To have a strong Family Time, you must include Scripture. Kids need to see that the Bible is real, valuable, and useful for their own lives. That's why sharing Scripture is the second ingredient in the Deuteronomy 6 passage that God gives for passing the faith on to kids. When you read the Bible to your children, you want them to know that it's different from any other book. At the end of the story, take a moment and ask, "What's the lesson learned?" We don't just read the Bible for entertainment, although it's captivating. Rather, the Bible is God's message to us, and one never knows what will happen when Scripture is heard or read. Hebrews 4:12 says, "For the word of God is living and active. Sharper than any double-edged sword, it penetrates even to dividing soul and spirit, joints and marrow; it judges the thoughts and attitudes of the heart."

Before you open the Bible, you might say with anticipation in your voice, "Son, I'm about to open the Bible. Are you ready? It's alive, and I'm not sure what will happen when I open it. But I know that this book is powerful. It changes our hearts. Today may be the day that God convicts me to apologize to someone for something I said that was hurtful. Or God might speak to me in the next few minutes about something important he wants me to do. Today God may reveal a new aspect about his love for me. I don't know what he's going to say to you or to me, but I'm about to open up God's Word to find out."

Reading the Bible is a time of excitement and anticipation. Sometimes God simply confirms his love or reminds us of his character and grace. Other times he prompts us to action or places a burden on our hearts to think differently or change something about the way we live. You never know what might happen when you open God's Word.

The word *devotions* in some families means sitting around a table and reading a passage of Scripture. Although some children may find that approach helpful, it's very adultlike, and often doesn't take into account the fact that God made kids to wiggle and be silly. Why not use silliness to your advantage and movement to teach God's Word? Passing the faith on to your children involves sharing Scripture in a way that takes their development and needs into account.

It probably isn't best to call your devotions a "quiet time." You may have a quiet time as an adult to ponder God and his

Word, but for kids, Family Time is usually not quiet. It's bubbly, interactive, and engaging.

One mom said, "We can't have devotions together as a family because our kids are too silly."

I (Scott) replied, "Are you saying that your kids are living and active?"

"Yes, that's the problem," she replied.

I said, "That's not a problem. That's an asset. In fact, those are the same words that describe the Bible in Hebrews 4:12. The Bible is living and active."

Add a little creativity to your devotions and you'll be just like Jesus, engaging people and passing the faith on to them. Teens benefit from logical discussions involving biblical passages, but they also appreciate it when the lesson is illustrated in practical ways. As much as it may seem that your teens don't want to be with you, teens really do want to know what their parents think, and they want their parents to know what they think too.

In one family Dad determined to create a commentary on the book of Proverbs with his teenage sons. They would read a chapter and then ask the question, "What verse in that chapter might we add to our pages?" They would identify a verse about a particular subject, such as listening, money, or anger, and then Dad would say, "What's the lesson we learn from that verse?"

Spread out on the dining room table were about twenty-five different pieces of paper, each with a title at the top, representing a subject referred to in the book of Proverbs. There were pages dedicated to anger, friends, money, wisdom, speech, and many more topics. One of the page headings was "The Immoral Woman," and whenever Proverbs had something to say about that subject, the boys took notice, and they wrote down the lessons learned. They were very interested in that subject, and the conversations about sexuality and moral purity made a lasting impact.

That commentary was never published, although it would have been a special book. Maybe it would have been called *A Commentary on the Book of Proverbs, by a Dad and His Sons*. But it was published in the hearts of those boys. They learned to love God's Word and to value the book of Proverbs and the wisdom it provides.

When you regularly pull out the Bible in family life, you teach children a very important lesson, that the Scriptures are our authority for life. The Bible is our standard and has answers for addressing the challenges we face every day.

> The Bible is our standard and has answers for addressing the challenges we face every day.

Over the past several years, there's been an explosion in the number of children's Bibles. These Bibles have pictures, illustrations, and age-appropriate communication styles. They engage children with the Scriptures, helping them realize that the Bible is relevant for them now. It's exciting and practical for their daily living. The reason you want to purchase age-appropriate Bibles for your children is to communicate that the Scriptures are for them now and apply to their lives. It's not just a book that they'll find interesting when they get to be adults.

One grandpa told this story: "I bought an early reader Bible for my six-year-old grandson. He immediately opened it up to the story of Moses and the burning bush and started to read the words on the page. He couldn't read them all, so I helped him, but it was clearly a text designed for children who were just learning how to read. My grandson loved the fact that he could read the Bible. He held that book tight in his arms and proclaimed, 'This is my Bible.'"

The Bible Helps Counter Wrong Thinking

One of the goals parents have is to change some of the erroneous beliefs their kids have in their hearts. For example, some kids believe that "when my brother is annoying, I have the right to punch him." Or, "If I'm unhappy with life situations, I can display my displeasure with whining, complaining, or a bad attitude." Or, "My job description in life is to have fun, and anything that looks like work should be avoided at all cost." These beliefs create tension in family relationships, and kids need to make some changes. It's amazing how many areas of a child's thinking can be corrected by looking at God's Word. The study of the Bible is practical, and kids learn valuable lessons about daily life when parents share the Scriptures with them.

In the Jackson family, Dad and Mom were disheartened by the competition and comparison between their sons, Jamal, age eight, and Desmond, age nine. They often raced to sit in the best seat in the van or wanted the first turn at the computer. Dad and Mom decided to read them the story of the two guys in the Bible who wanted the best seat. Mark 10 tells the story. James and John came to Jesus and said, "Let one of us sit at your right and the other at your left in your glory" (v. 37). Jesus' answer to them was, "Whoever wants to become great among you must be your servant, and whoever wants to be first must be slave of all" (vv. 43–44).

Dad and Mom then created the "Upside Down Game" to illustrate this biblical truth in a playful way. They had a race to see who could serve others the most in a five-minute period, and they kept track with points on a piece of paper. Dad said to Mom, "I just want to tell you how pretty you are." Dad got a point. Mom got up and started to rub Dad's shoulders. She got a point. The boys then joined in, first with Dad and Mom, and then with each other. Jamal said, "Desmond, you're really good at baseball." Jamal got a point. The game was enjoyable, and when the time was up, they talked about the value of service and putting others first. Not only was it a fun family experience, but it also generated a different way of thinking for the boys over the next few days. Dad and Mom were able to talk about having an attitude of servanthood instead of wanting to be first or best.

The goal is to pass the faith on to kids so that they'll put biblical truths into practice. The Scriptures take root in a child's heart, equipping the conscience and guiding a child's internal motivations. But how is faith developed in the life of a child? God gives the answer in Romans 10:17: "Faith comes from hearing the message, and the message is heard through the word of Christ." As parents open the Bible regularly with their children and talk about the lessons learned from God's Word, a child's faith begins to grow. It's nurtured through more Bible stories and applications to the child's life. A constant diet of the Scriptures provides children with a way to think about themselves, about God, and about their purpose in life.

> The Scriptures take root in a child's heart, equipping the conscience and guiding a child's internal motivations.

If you go to the doctor, he might give you a prescription and tell you, "Take this pill once a day and come back and see me in a week." You may not get well the first day, but by the end of a period of faithful, daily treatment, wellness is achieved. A similar thing can happen in our spiritual lives when we immerse ourselves in God's Word on a regular basis. The Bible isn't a quick fix. It provides deep, long-lasting solutions for life. If, for example, you're having troubles and challenges, you might read about heaven in Revelation 21–22 every day for a week and see what impact it has on your heart. Meditating on heaven can help us get our minds on spiritual things and give us a new perspective on life's challenges.

If your child has a problem with selfishness, then it would certainly be helpful to do some teaching about the biblical concept of honor. It's important to be careful about overusing God's Word in correction so that a child doesn't develop a punitive picture of God. Often, presenting the solutions from God's Word in a positive way gives children a vision for something better. It may be that memorizing Romans 12:10 ("Honor one another above yourselves") or Philippians 2:3–4 ("Do nothing out of selfish ambition or vain conceit, but in humility consider others better than yourselves. Each of you should look not only to your own interests, but also to the interests of others") is just the therapy that helps bring about a positive change in your child.

God's Word is relevant, and every area of family life provides opportunities for its application. The Bible contains the secret ingredients children need to be successful in life, both now and for their futures. That's why it's so important for parents to spend time learning God's Word themselves and then passing the truths on to their children. Using fun, activity, and play helps kids receive the truths.

The Family Challenge encourages spontaneous integration of the Bible with life, but by taking the challenge, you also agree to at least one planned time per week. A scheduled Family Time of twenty to thirty minutes of fun devotions can open the door for many spontaneous conversations to apply that same truth for weeks to come.

Consider taking the Family Challenge. Schedule a regular time once a week to intentionally pass the faith on to your kids. As you build relationship, share Scripture, and practice faith, you'll see the difference in your family. Your kids will begin to think and act differently. It's encouraging to watch children grow in God's grace. At the heart of spiritual growth is an understanding of God's Word. Your commitment to God and his Word in your family will have a marked effect on you and your kids for the rest of their lives.

15

Practicing Faith Teaches That It's Real

If grasping faith for kids is like learning to drive, then the church is the classroom and the home is behind the wheel.

Faith is practical. It results in action. Faith forms the basis for our lives, both as children and as adults. Faith isn't just Bible lessons learned at church. It isn't just encouragement that helps us get through the day. Faith is the foundation we build our lives upon. It affects everything we do. It's more than just mental assent or head knowledge. Faith is our life. That's why God included it as the third ingredient in Deuteronomy 6:8–9 for passing the faith on to kids. Practicing faith means that it is integrated into life, not just read during a worship time or a devotional experience. God commanded the Israelites, "Tie them as symbols on your hands and bind them on your foreheads. Write them on the doorframes of your houses and on your gates." In other words, integrate them into your life.

Sometimes parents make the mistake of lecturing too much

to their kids. Some kids may respond well to that, but if your child is an experiential learner, you'll want to look for ways to use life experience to pass on God's truth. Faith must be practical for kids to grab hold of it. Parents pass the faith on to their children when they practice faith with them. The Christian life is more than words and teaching; it's action. When parents put faith into practice, it begins to live in their hearts. When parents practice faith with their children, it begins to live in the hearts of their children as well.

> Faith is the foundation we build our lives upon. It affects everything we do.

James 2:14 asks the question, "What good is it, my brothers, if a man claims to have faith but has no deeds?" A few verses later we learn the answer: "As the body without the spirit is dead, so faith without deeds is dead" (v. 26). It's important to put our faith to the test by applying it regularly to our lives. Faith works itself out in who we are.

But What if God Doesn't Answer My Child's Prayer?

When you take time to pray with your kids about life situations, they get to see the power of God at work. You don't have to be concerned that your kids will get discouraged because God doesn't give them exactly what they prayed for. Through prayer children learn that God isn't a genie. He's God. He wasn't created for our benefit to make us happy. We were created for him, and we seek to discover his will.

Practicing faith is done in many ways and takes on many faces. Ask yourself how you practice faith, and then invite your kids to participate with you. When a dad announces that he's learning to be more compassionate and looks for ways to show it to others, kids take notice. They see God actually working in Dad's heart. When a mom asks forgiveness for yelling at her son, he sees God active in his mom's heart. True faith in any of our lives changes how we live. It affects our actions and the way we think about life. Kids benefit from seeing that kind of faith in action.

Spiritual transparency can take place in the normal conversations of life. It may have been that in the past you saw a beautiful sunset, felt gratefulness to God, and shot up a prayer of admiration for his creativity and beauty. But it was done in private. Now you say it out loud, "God, that sure is a beautiful sunset you made." You're not trying to concoct something that isn't there. You're just revealing your spirituality to your children.

If you go back to Deuteronomy 6:20–21, you see one of the natural ways to practice faith with your kids: answer their questions using faith and your spiritual history. "In the future, when your son asks you, 'What is the meaning of the stipulations, decrees and laws the LORD our God has commanded you?' tell him . . ." The passage goes on to give spiritual history. Children often ask the questions, "Why?" "Why do I have to do this?" "Why are you saying no?" Just as it's okay for us to ask respectful questions of God, it's good for our children to learn to ask respectful questions of us.

When children ask questions, it's often a good time to share convictions, beliefs, and the legacy of your spiritual faith. Even if you've recently come to Christ, you can share about how important he is to you now and how you desire to serve him with all your heart.

You May Be Living Out the Bible More Than You Realize

Your family rules come from your convictions, and many of those convictions come straight from the Bible. Even those that don't are often examples of your desire to live out your faith. If you tell your son to come for dinner, and he, not wanting to stop his activity, says, "I'm not hungry," you now have an opportunity to teach about a conviction you have. His belief is that mealtime is simply for satisfying his appetite, and if he's not hungry, then coming to the table isn't necessary. You, on the other hand, believe that mealtime is more than that. You want your family together, and the social component of the meal is even more important than the food. Thus, your training in the moment provides the practical application your child needs to experience the faith. Your convictions demonstrate your value of family relationships.

You have reasons behind your rules, and each rule is a demonstration of your convictions. You clean up the house because of a sense of stewardship. Your family doesn't allow siblings to hit each other to solve problems because you want to teach kindness and more constructive forms of problem solving. You use manners to show honor to others and try to get somewhere on time to demonstrate your integrity.

As children live in your home, they're experiencing the rules of your family that come out of your convictions. But many times they see the rules and not what's behind them. This is a reality that's even difficult for many adults to understand. Regular discussions with your kids about the convictions behind the rules often reveal how you're living out your faith in daily life. Kids then can catch the reality of what it means to love God with all your heart, soul, mind, and strength, and love your neighbor as yourself.

You might say to your daughter who is headed out the door, "I'll be praying for you today as you try to work out that problem with your friend," or to your son as you leave for the office, "Son, would you please pray for me? I'm not feeling too well, and I have an important meeting at work." Those kinds of prayers acknowledge the need for God, but they also demonstrate that you're living every day in a way that relies on God's grace. You believe that he has answers and that he cares about you in the personal, daily needs of life.

> You have reasons behind your rules, and each rule is a demonstration of your convictions.

When Jesus was teaching his disciples to pray, he included these words, "Give us today our daily bread" (Matthew 6:11). That phrase implies the need to come to God regularly for his provision and care. Prayer not only changes others, but it changes us. When we pray for a grumpy neighbor, we often find ourselves more sensitive to his needs and patient when relating to him. As kids pray for help for a problem with a friend and ask for strength to get through a difficult project, they see God answer their prayers. This further strengthens their faith.

Praying Out Loud Is a Ministry to Others

Some parents feel uncomfortable praying out loud. They often view prayer as a private activity and their faith as very personal. Those things are true, but praying with others, especially children, is a great way to allow kids to experience the grace of God themselves. One mom said, "I realized that I was limiting our family's spiritual growth because of my fear of praying out loud. I determined to get over it, and praying with my kids proved to be the training ground I needed. I was so touched by the simple, real prayers of my children that I was able to pray out loud with them. Now I feel much more comfortable praying in a group of adults when the opportunity arises. I realized that it's not about having the right words. It's about connecting my heart to God."

Some parents develop good habits of praying before meals

or before bed. Those are great exercises of faith, but be careful that you have other times when you talk about prayer and God's Word. You don't want your children to believe that God only shows up at mealtime and bedtime. God is ever present and eagerly seeks relationship with us.

> You don't want your children to believe that God only shows up at mealtime and bedtime.

One dad had his watch beep every hour for a while. His kids asked him why he was doing that. His answer was, "I want to remind myself that my time is God's time, so every time it beeps, I just say a short prayer to God, thanking him for this next hour. It helps me be ready for the interruptions that often happen around here. Instead of getting frustrated with them, now I try to look at the interruptions as opportunities in one way or another, and sometimes they're God's way of getting my attention."

When children watch their parents trying to live out their faith, good things happen. That doesn't mean we have to be perfect. Kids can learn from our imperfections as well. Saying, "I'm sorry" to a child demonstrates humility. Admitting that you're working on something in your life, such as keeping calm under pressure, is helpful for kids to see. The family is a laboratory for growth for parents and for their kids. Offering and receiving grace is a demonstration of faith and helps children integrate their spiritual lives into the rest of who they are.

Serving Others Is Faith in Action

Another way parents can practice faith is by serving others outside the family. Giving money, time, or energy can help kids learn to think about others and not just their own needs. In one family, the parents responded to a desire their son had to serve.

This young boy heard about disease and suffering in Africa and wanted to help provide clean drinking water for the people there. The family asked for permission to set up a table at their church and raised money to give to an organization that built wells in villages that didn't have clean water.

Looking for opportunities to work together to serve others is a practical way to demonstrate faith. It's surprising how many children actually develop an internal motivation to please the Lord because of the meaningful service they do with their families. Serving in a soup kitchen, visiting a nursing home, sending gifts to a missionary, or shoveling snow off a neighbor's sidewalk are all ways to live out your faith with your children.

Sometimes the family can become rather self-focused with so many activities complicating the schedule. Although kids benefit from activity and events, sometimes they develop the impression that life is all about them, their needs, their development, and their accomplishments. It's good to give to others, and the earlier children learn that, the better. When we give money, time, and talents, we give a bit of our own selfishness away in the process. It's part of God's design for giving.

As you plan your family's time, be careful that you don't allow it to plan you. Busyness is one of the main reasons parents don't spend time passing the faith on to their kids. When you take control of your schedule, you allow margin that often can be used in productive ways. When you take the Family Challenge, you set aside a particular period of time for the Lord as a family. It may be only twenty or thirty minutes a week, but that strategic time can produce a powerful impact on your children's lives. In addition, you'll learn to live out your faith spontaneously in visible, practical ways. Thus, you'll be intentional about passing the faith on to kids through building relationship, sharing Scripture, and practicing faith.

16

Prepare for Resistance

If kids learn about the faith, they think
it's interesting. If they learn how to
practice faith, they see that it's real.

M arsha's story is so inspiring that we want to share it with
you. Starting Family Time in her home wasn't easy at
first. She experienced a lot of resistance, but she did several
things that kept her focused. Her persistance and hard work are
admirable and provide encouragement for all of us.

I have four kids, ages fourteen, eleven, nine, and three, so my
first challenge was to figure out how to do Family Time with
all of them. I try to have one scheduled Bible time a week, and
I involve my fourteen-year-old in the leadership of it. That
keeps him engaged most of the time.

But over time we've faced challenges of busyness, bad
attitudes, and just fatigue. We've been doing Family Time,
though, now for over two years, and it's a part of who we are.
We find ourselves missing the times together when other
things come up. I'm pleased with our progress, but it's a

continual challenge to make spiritual interaction in our family a priority.

Leadership takes on many forms and faces. If you're trying to pass the faith on to your children, then you're exerting spiritual leadership in your home. Whether you're male, female, a grandparent, an adoptive parent, a stepparent, or a foster parent, you can have a significant impact on the spiritual growth of the children in your care.

Some parents, however, get discouraged in their leadership, resulting in a loss of determination and energy to accomplish the task. The purpose of this chapter is to help you address that discouragement before it happens. All leaders experience resistance. If you're ready for it, you'll be able to hang in there, especially when things get tough.

God's Grace Is Powerful

Marsha continued,

> The greatest form of encouragement comes from God's grace working in and through me. It's important for me to regularly stand under the spigot of God's grace, especially in times of need. It's amazing how a strong prayer life, regularly reading the Word, and the encouragement of other believers become conduits of God's grace to help in times of pressure. God often provides spiritual resources when emotional reserves are low.

We appreciate Marsha's honesty and spiritual transparency. The reality is that resistance often comes from three different sources. Recognizing the cause can often target your prayers and prepare you to persevere even after you feel like quitting. The first source of resistance comes from inside you. Good intentions often facilitate a strong start to a new venture, but it isn't long until the newness wears off and the hard work begins. It's in those moments that convictions are put to the test. A variety of internal issues can hinder effectiveness, so it's important to be ready in advance to address them.

Before you start leading, it would be helpful for you to set reasonable goals and write them down. A clearly defined, practical objective is necessary to keep you on track as you hit the speed bumps along the way. You might, for example, determine to have one Family Time each week for twenty to thirty minutes and look for at least two more spontaneous conversations with your children. Keep a log of your progress. If you miss a week, determine to do better the next week. It's encouraging and motivating to look back at a journal to see what success you had in the past.

> It's encouraging and motivating to look back to a journal to see what success you had in the past.

On the first page of that journal, write down your plan, but also jot down a few of the reasons why you're doing it. Marsha wrote this in her journal: "My plan is to organize one Family Time each week and to look for one spiritual conversation each day with at least one of my children. I want to do this for three reasons. (1) I believe that the success of my children is, to a large degree, determined by their spiritual strength. (2) I love God and want to serve him in my home. (3) I want to model godliness and allow my family to hold me spiritually accountable for my own growth." As Marsha read those words a couple of times a week, she was continually reminded of her reasons and found encouragement to continue on.

Resistance from Your Family

A second source of resistance comes from others in the home. The problem, however, isn't so much your mate or your children. It has to do with your expectations. Change takes time. In Marsha's case, her husband traveled a lot and couldn't participate in the Family Time very often. When he was home, she would try to get him involved, but for the most part she took on the challenge and the leadership for her family. Her husband appreciated that, and he supported her and participated when he could. Marsha affirmed any initiative he did have in their spiritual relationships and encouraged him to be a spiritual leader in their home.

In addition to getting parents on the same page, it's important to realize that children have their own ideas of what they want to do with their time and energy. Life doesn't always go as planned. Things happen. So set your goal, but be flexible in your expectations. Some weeks will flow more easily than others. If you're experiencing resistance from your kids on a regular basis, you may need to change your approach. Maybe in your home an evening Family Time isn't the best. One dad told us that when they shifted to a Saturday morning activity, his kids were more responsive.

> Things happen. So set your goal, but be flexible in your expectations.

On the other hand, sometimes resistance on the part of a child is an indication of selfishness requiring some discipline or training. A child might change what could have been a great family experience into a time of correction because of a bad attitude or self-centeredness. Flexibility in parenting contributes to success. Do the necessary discipline, and then come back to the Family Time later or another day. Sometimes the best conversation of a week can come during correction, so remember that your plans may not be the only way God wants to work in a given day or situation.

Spiritual Warfare Is Real

A third type of resistance comes in the form of spiritual attack. We know that Satan hinders progress in a family in a variety of ways. Ephesians 4:26–27 says, "In your anger do not sin: Do not let the sun go down while you are still angry, and do not give the devil a foothold." Emotional intensity is often a way that Satan hinders spiritual progress. But that's only one of his schemes. He loves to derail progress, kill spiritual growth, and hinder closeness in a family. The best way to fight Satan's attack is to use the spiritual resources provided by God himself, including prayer and the truth of his Word.

Don't let discouragement hinder your forward progress. Expect resistance and be prepared for it. Your attitude can make all the difference. When you base your motivation on your convictions instead of on results, you're able to do what needs to be done even when things get hard.

Jared told us this story:

> I know that God wants me to be the spiritual leader in my home. My wife and I determined to prepare fun and interesting lessons at mealtimes and just before bed. The first few evenings it went quite well, but then I found myself in a season where I had to work late, and for several days in a row we weren't able to connect with our kids the way we wanted as a family. My wife tried to do it on her own, but she found it much harder without me.
>
> I would come home tired, or we were transporting our

kids to baseball until late, so things just didn't happen as planned. My wife and I decided to try a different approach for a while. We changed to afternoon after church and sent each of our kids on a mission in the morning to bring back to our family a lesson learned that they could share with us. The change in approach worked, and our kids helped lead our Family Times. When our schedule settled down again, we were able to go back to our dinner and bedtime discussions. The variety was necessary for our schedule but also kept Family Time new and interesting.

One of the benefits we found is that our children were initiating more spontaneously with us. They seem to be creating the spontaneous times based on our planned times together. Family Time for us doesn't always happen on a schedule, but it does happen. That's the important thing for us. We're seeing God work in our marriage and in our kids, and we're convinced that one of the things that's making our family stronger is our determination to grow spiritually.

Jared and his family will be successful. It's not necessarily a technique that makes spiritual closeness grow. It's the general attitude that sharing spiritually is important and that somehow, in the midst of our busy lives, we're going to make sure it happens.

Pressing On

Some children seem to be more receptive spiritually than others, even in the same family. Marsha told us this story:

My two sons love our devotion times and seem eager to enter in as we pray and learn things from the Bible. But my daughter, Kaylie, is more resistant. It makes me sad to see her drift off during our times or want to quickly get on to other things that seem more important to her.

I've had to do extra work to try to connect with Kaylie spiritually. Since she loves to spend time alone with me, I thought that might be an opportunity to connect. She does respond more one-on-one, but I still don't see the same enthusiasm I see in my boys.

The other day, though, I got a glimmer of hope when a teacher from church reported an encouraging story. She told me that Kaylie had corrected a fellow student and taken a stand for what's right when one of the other girls was being mean to a friend. We had been talking at home about meanness and the value of friends, so the report confirmed that something had actually made an impact on Kaylie. I have a feeling that I'll have to give a lot more time to Kaylie's spiritual growth than I will to the boys. I'm recognizing more and more that parenting is a walk of faith and that I can't control the ultimate outcomes. I'm just one of the tools God uses to influence my children. I'm honored to be part of what he's doing in my kids and want to find more and more ways to do my part well.

Being a Godly Influence

Marsha is right. The work you do as a parent doesn't serve to ultimately control children or to magically determine an outcome. You're only influencing your children for God's purposes. It's God who ultimately changes your children's hearts. But the daily work you do with your kids prepares the soil for the seeds to grow. Your faithfulness in the face of what appears to be little progress is often the tool God uses to provide a strong witness in your child's life that will be remembered for years to come.

So, when the winds of resistance come into your life, hang in there, be faithful, and do what God wants you to do, no matter what the response. Remember, your primary job is to serve God no matter what the cost. Galatians 6:9 says, "Let us not become weary in doing good, for at the proper time we will reap a harvest if we do not give up." Even when the results don't seem obvious, God is working. If everything always turned out the way you wanted, then you wouldn't need faith. Parenting is one of the greatest walks of faith that anyone can ever take. The results are often seen years down the road. The most important thing is that you obey God and do what he has called you to do.

> Remember, your primary job is to serve God no matter what the cost.

Every parent is a spiritual leader in the home. Husbands and fathers have that special, God-given leadership role, but that doesn't mean that moms sit back and only support or wait until their husbands lead. It's often the initiative of a wife that provides the helpful encouragement to a husband that spiritual training is reasonable, fun, and meaningful. Taking initiative is a leadership quality. Whether you view yourself as a leader or not, your influence on your child's spiritual health is significant.

It's also amazing how much influence a grandparent, stepparent, or foster parent can have on a child's spiritual development. Perseverance is essential. Your excitement about God is contagious. Kids are developing morally and spiritually, and your influence is often significant. You can pass a godly heritage on to the children in your life, no matter what your role in the family, but it takes continual initiative. When you embrace a strong conviction and a commitment in your heart that God wants you to exert spiritual influence in their lives, you'll help pass on a legacy for the future.

Don't skip the next chapter because your child has already made a commitment to Christ. A childhood conversion is powerful, but it must be nurtured, or children feel as if they've grown out of the faith. A relationship with Christ is dynamic, not just an event in one's history. Look for ways to nurture your child's faith, and the experience with Christ will be one that's ongoing.

17

Leading a Child
to Christ

The most important influence on a child's
heart isn't education. It's salvation.

G od doesn't have any grandchildren," Mom said to her
eleven-year-old son.

"What does that mean?" he asked curiously.

Mom used the question to open up the dialogue again about
the importance of a personal commitment to Christ. She continued, "It means that every person, young or old, must come to
Jesus and make a personal commitment to him."

How old can a child be to make that commitment? What
does it entail? What if a child doesn't understand what he or she
is really committing to? All those are good questions and important ones to consider as you help your child make a personal
commitment to Jesus.

The Conscience Leads a Person to Salvation

The conscience provides a sensitivity to right and wrong. Initiative gives kids the character needed to respond to the promptings of the conscience and the Holy Spirit. The most important of those promptings is the call to accept Jesus Christ as one's personal Lord and Savior. The greatest initiative one can take is to follow Jesus. The most effective form of internal motivation is to please God. All people, young and old, can put themselves into the Bible story of Jesus walking by the side of the Sea of Galilee. The Bible tells us in Mark 1:16–18, "As Jesus walked beside the Sea of Galilee, he saw Simon and his brother Andrew casting a net into the lake, for they were fishermen. 'Come, follow me,' Jesus said, 'and I will make you fishers of men.' At once they left their nets and followed him." Even children can make that personal decision to follow Christ, prompted by God's grace and the drawing of the Holy Spirit in their hearts.

Romans 10:9 gives helpful direction on how a person gets saved: "If you confess with your mouth, 'Jesus is Lord,' and believe in your heart that God raised him from the dead, you will be saved." Two essential ingredients form the basis for salvation. One is an outward statement, and the other is an internal commitment. Many children make decisions for Christ as kids. In fact, some people who grow up in a home where Christ is served can't identify a particular event or moment when they committed themselves to the Lord. They grew up in that understanding of the faith and eagerly serve him with their whole hearts today. Other children can remember a specific moment when Christ became very real to them, and they mark that prayer as their conversion experience.

Praying a sinner's prayer is a clear way of expressing one's need for salvation and a desire to invite God to live in one's heart. When a child is ready to pray such a prayer, you can encourage that moment, mark it on a calendar, and celebrate it. But a prayer by itself isn't enough. Sometimes children get caught up in the emotion and pray a prayer that they aren't ready to follow through on. Faith is nurtured over time, and the daily commitment to Christ and continual teaching of what it means to serve him produce greater steps of heart change.

One man, reflecting on his spiritual development, reports his story this way: "When I was just three years old, I committed my heart to Jesus Christ. I remember the exact place and time. I was at a Bible club for kids, and we were having a story about the need to be part of God's family. Our class was in the choir loft of the church. I was moved by the story, and when the leader asked who wanted to accept Jesus, I responded. The leader led me in a prayer, and that was it. I don't remember much else. But I look back at that decision as my conversion experience. Since then I've made other commitments of my heart to Christ, but that first childhood conversion was a starting point that I consider my spiritual awakening."

> Sometimes children get caught up in the emotion and pray a prayer that they aren't ready to follow through on.

Kids Comprehend Salvation Differently at Each Developmental Stage

As children go through developmental stages, their ability to understand increases. Obviously a three-year-old child can't understand atonement, crucifixion, and the cost of discipleship. But a young child can trust, experience guilt for sin, and want to be part of God's family. In fact, adults can make conversion a rather complicated experience. It was Jesus who tried to counteract the religious system created by the Pharisees and teach his disciples about the heart. In Mark 10:15, he said, "I tell you the truth, anyone who will not receive the kingdom of God like a little child will never enter it."

> Adults can make conversion a rather complicated experience.

A childlike faith is necessary for anyone, young or old, to receive salvation. Simple trust in Jesus and a willingness to follow him and invite him to come into the heart are the essence of salvation. As children grow and develop, they learn more about what that commitment entails.

One pastor told his story:

I made a childhood conversion, and with the help of my parents and a good children's program at my church, that faith was nurtured over many years. But I remember when I was fourteen years old, and a youth leader challenged my personal faith in a new way that I hadn't experienced before. At that moment I knew I needed to commit myself to Christ again. It's not that my early commitment was ineffective. It's just that at age fourteen I understood more about what Christ wanted for me, and I wanted to rise to the occasion. The story continued for me as, years later, I went to seminary and took a whole class on soteriology, the study of salvation. During that class I developed a tremendous appreciation for what God had done for me through Christ. I remember saying to myself, "Wow! I didn't know all this when I was a young child and made a commitment. I wonder if I was really saved back then." But then I realized that at several points in my life, I've come to appreciate God more, and at each point of discovery, I've responded to God again. It's not so much the depth of knowledge that one needs for salvation. It's the responsiveness of the human heart.

Some children who make a decision for Christ later want to rededicate their lives to God. Often that's because they feel as though they drifted away from him for a while and now want to reconnect. Those are good decisions that parents can nurture. It doesn't mean that the early decision was inadequate. It's just a sign of growing dedication and spiritual awareness. Of course, some children say the right words or pray a prayer when they're young and it really wasn't a heart commitment. Those children particularly benefit from a recommitment experience with Jesus.

Salvation is both an event and a process. It's an event because there is a particular time when a person commits to Christ. Some may not remember a specific day, but there was a sense of desire and commitment that existed early on. Salvation is also a process. One can't rely on a past prayer as the sole statement of his or her spirituality. Growth takes place over time. If a child isn't serving Jesus or doesn't have a sensitivity to spiritual things, then likely another conversion experience of some sort will take place.

One dad communicated the idea of following Christ to his thirteen-year-old son this way: "Son, do you hear God calling you?"

His son looked puzzled. "What do you mean?"

"The Bible says that God calls us. That's not just about a decision we make once in our lives, but the calling of God has a forward look to it. Philippians 3:14 says, 'I press on toward the goal to win the prize for which God has called me heavenward in Christ Jesus.' God has certainly called us to trust him as our Savior, but he also is calling us to live the life of grace. I like to picture God calling out the way to me or giving me a map that guides my continual movement during my day and week. God is like our GPS, directing us throughout the day."

Later that week Dad had forgotten the conversation, but his son referred back to it by saying, "I think God is calling me to be a professional baseball player."

Dad smiled and said, "I'm glad you're listening to the Lord, son. I don't know whether he will have you be a professional baseball player or not, but if he does, how will you serve him in that role?" The important thing for Dad was that the dialogue continued. Whether professional sports is in his child's future or not isn't the most important thing. Rather, learning to listen to God and trust him each day will provide the long-term guidance necessary for his son.

A problem happens when children, or their parents, overly rely on a prayer or a past spiritual experience instead of living for Jesus now. The lifestyle of service for Jesus is ongoing and can be nurtured in family life as children progress through developmental stages. A child may commit to Christ as a preschooler and then learn new things during the elementary years that enlarge that faith. Ongoing dedication of one's life is necessary during those years as new understanding takes place about what it means to serve Jesus and what salvation is all about. The same is true when kids hit the teen years. Parents can do a lot to help children bring their faith into adolescence instead of leaving it behind in childhood. When children launch into adulthood, they'll need guidance about what it means to carry their faith with them.

It's Important to Nurture a Child's Faith Through the Years

Intellectual, emotional, and spiritual development all bring children into new ways of thinking about God, Jesus, and the Christian life. Your interaction with your children about spiritual things at various stages helps them see that faith is essential, not childish. When children integrate their faith into their lives over multiple developmental stages, that faith embeds itself more fully into the human heart.

According to Romans 10:9, mentioned earlier, salvation has two components: confession with the mouth and belief in the heart. Parents are especially effective in helping their children understand the underlying truths that make salvation necessary and possible. Kids can understand sin, guilt, and forgiveness. They can understand love, sacrifice, and being part of a family. As children get a bit older, they can understand how truly big the sacrifice of God's love is and how payment for our sin is such a significant and necessary gift. Some children are motivated to come to Christ because of a fear of hell, others because they want to go to heaven when they die. Still others want to be part of God's family, just like mom and dad. Yet others are so overwhelmed with gratefulness for God's provision in salvation that they're drawn to a personal commitment.

The conscience plays a critical role in the salvation process. It's often the prompter that increases the desire for salvation in one's heart. A child may experience guilt and recognize a need for a Savior. Or he may simply want to do what's right, and salvation is one of those steps he feels are important. Some children want to belong and are prompted by the conscience's need to care about others. Each person is different, but the conscience influences the desire to come to Christ. Hebrews 10:22 describes what happens to the conscience when one gets saved: "Let us draw near to God with a sincere heart in full assurance of faith, having our hearts sprinkled to cleanse us from a guilty conscience and having our bodies washed with pure water." The salvation experience touches the heart in a way that even affects one's conscience.

> The conscience plays a critical role in the salvation process.

As you work with your kids, you'll want to be teaching them about God and his plan while at the same time encouraging them to choose God for themselves. It's a personal decision and the most important commitment one will ever make.

Guiding Kids to Trust Christ as Savior

You never know when God will do a significant work in your child's heart. It may take place during or after a crisis, following a meaningful teaching time at church, or while simply listening to a Bible story and being asked a personal question. But at some point, your prayer that your child will invite Jesus into his heart may be met with a yes. When that happens, what will you do? Here are some important things to remember as you lead your child to Christ.

1. *Your attitude should be welcoming, encouraging, and excited.* Those parents who use fear to motivate kids often hinder spiritual development because of a misunderstanding of God. If your child is responding to Jesus to avoid hell, that's okay, but you'll want to emphasize

God's love and provision along with any discussion of the evil of sin.

2. *Pray.* You want your child to communicate directly with God. You might say, "I'm glad you want to ask Jesus into your life. Let's pray; you can do that right now." If your child is hesitant or doesn't know what to say, you might have the child repeat after you or maybe just coach your child by saying something like, "Why don't you talk to God yourself. Just tell him that you know you are a sinner and that you are grateful that Jesus is your Savior and that you want to invite Jesus into your heart." Children often have the sweetest prayers when given the chance to talk to God on their own.

3. *Nurture that commitment.* Have your child share it with others. Talk about what it means to follow Jesus now in the small things of life. Read the Bible, and look for practical applications in the stories to further demonstrate a life that follows Jesus. Part of what you're doing is helping your child develop an identity as a Christ-follower.

4. *Continue to look for spiritually sensitive moments and encourage greater commitment to Christ.* Although one decision is meaningful, ongoing submission to God is necessary for everyone. You might even talk about your own desire and need for fellowship with God, confession of sin, and reliance on the Holy Spirit in your life.

Baptism and Communion

Baptism and communion are privileges that belong to God's covenant people. Talk with your child about what they mean and why they're important. One dad said, "Each time we celebrate the Lord's Table at church, I have my kids sit with me. I tell them that they can't participate in communion unless they're near me so that we can do it as a family. It's not a play time, but a serious time to remember Christ's sacrifice for our sin. My kids have grown in the understanding of communion, and it's a special time for them."

Helping children come to a personal faith in Jesus Christ is an important part of their development. For some children this commitment is easier than for others. Your discussion of faith and practice of it in your home will prepare their hearts for a decision at some point. Practice spirituality regularly by having children pray, read the Bible, and serve God even before they have expressed that personal commitment. Teach them daily to follow Jesus, and that training will prepare the way for them to choose him on their own. Talk about the importance of each person making a decision for Christ. No one gets to heaven because of a friend's faith or a parent's love. Salvation comes through a personal faith in Jesus Christ as Lord and Savior.

Remember that God is the one who draws a person to himself. It's God's grace that even allows an individual to have a desire to get saved. That's why it's so important to be praying for your child. Pray for that time of personal commitment. Pray for a soft heart and a sensitivity to the Holy Spirit's work. And pray that God will give you wisdom to do your part in the spiritual development of your child.

But choosing Jesus as one's Savior is only one step of spiritual growth, and it isn't even the first one. Many spiritual interactions and much teaching and training usually take place before that decision happens. Once the child makes a commitment to

Christ, there's still much work to do in the areas of discipleship and practicing faith. But as you nurture your child's spiritual growth, you have a powerful ally. We'll discuss that in the next chapter.

18

Children and the Holy Spirit

The conscience and the Holy Spirit are
both inside the human heart of believers.
The first will prompt you to do what's right.
The second will empower you to do it.

Lance, at age fourteen, struggled with anxiety. He described his problem this way: "I worried a lot about the safety of our home. I would check the doors and windows several times a day. I knew it was a problem, and I wanted to change."

The words "I want to change" were just what Mom was waiting for. She contacted a local Christian counselor, and the three of them determined to work on the problem together. After just a couple of months of work, Lance and his mom were encouraged by the tremendous improvement.

When asked, "What helped you the most?" Lance replied, "It was a greater understanding about the Holy Spirit at work in my life. I used to think of the Holy Spirit living in me, but being quiet and off in a corner somewhere. Now I realize that my body is his temple, and he is actively moving around inside of me. The verses about the fruit of the Spirit were helpful because I realized that God gives me peace, love, and joy, and he does it when I let him. So I've been letting him do that more. I feel like there's a factory inside of me where God wants to make good feelings to replace my bad feelings. When I focus more on what the Holy Spirit wants for me, it just gives me something I didn't have before."

Can a child be filled with the Holy Spirit? What a great question, and its answer propels us to a new dimension of empowering children with a sense of internal motivation, one that is supernatural. Teaching kids about the Holy Spirit and training them to rely on him can help them overcome all kinds of challenges.

> "I used to think of the Holy Spirit living in me, but being quiet and off in a corner somewhere."

Let's first start by making a distinction between spiritual maturity and spirituality. Spiritual maturity is on a continuum. You can always find someone who is more or less spiritually mature than you are. Spiritual maturity involves one's ability to trust God in challenging situations; manage temptations, emotions, and desires; and utilize biblical truths in daily life. Spiritual maturity grows over time as one gets to know God, responds to his leadership, and applies biblical truth as a lifestyle. Children can grow in their own spiritual maturity through prayer, Bible study, service, and being mentored in the Christian life.

Spirituality, however, is different and simply means being filled with the Spirit. In fact, any one person can be just as spiritual as someone else at any moment. Spirituality is not on a continuum but rather is all-or-nothing. You can't be filled with the Spirit just a little. You either are or you aren't at this moment in time. To be filled with the Spirit means that you're yielding your heart to God right now at this moment.

Imagine two circles. One represents being Spirit-filled, and the other represents being what God calls "worldly" or "carnal." First Corinthians 3:1 says, "Brothers and sisters, I could not address you as people who live by the Spirit but as people who are still worldly." At any moment you are either controlled by the Spirit or controlled by the flesh. Many good things can be done in the flesh, but there's something powerful about being led by the Holy Spirit. The verse continues, describing their level of spiritual maturity as being "mere infants in Christ." The reality for anyone is that the more you live empowered by the Spirit, the more you grow spiritually.

A person who is filled with the Holy Spirit is someone who is at that moment allowing the Holy Spirit to lead. When individuals take control of their own lives, they're acting in the flesh, a state the Bible calls "worldly." That's why Ephesians 5:18 says, "Be [*continually*] filled with the Holy Spirit." The word *continually* is added there but is implied by the verb tense used in the passage. Anyone who wants to be filled with the Holy Spirit must continually turn their will over to God.

How does this all apply to children? You may find a Happy Meal at McDonald's or a children's menu at your favorite restaurant, but you won't find a child-size portion of the Holy Spirit. The same Holy Spirit who empowers adults is available to children as well. When anyone receives Jesus Christ as Lord and Savior, he or she also receives "the Holy Spirit who lives in us" (2 Timothy 1:14). We know that a child can yield his will to a parent and follow a parent's lead. In fact, one of the main reasons parents teach obedience to their children is to prepare them to obey God.

Children become more able to respond to outside leadership at different developmental stages; some of them can even become aware of and submit to God early on. Whenever you talk about God with kids, whatever their ages, make sure that you're keeping a balance between respect for God because he is righteous, holy, and judges people, and the loving leadership of God, which provides strength, encouragement, and direction. Too much of one or the other can result in a skewed understanding of who God is.

One dad realized that he was overusing the Bible in correction, and his son was developing an opinion of God as harsh. Dad made a change in his approach and spent more time talking about God's grace and how God gives it freely to those who seek it, to provide the spiritual strength needed to handle challenges—like an annoying brother or an unreasonable coach.

When working in counseling with a child, one of my (Scott) favorite questions to ask is, "Are you a Christian?" The child often looks at me puzzled as if to say, "Why are you asking me that? I thought we were supposed to be working on my anger or my relationship with my mom." It's then that I talk about the distinct benefits that come for a person who has made a commitment to Christ. That person has the Holy Spirit residing inside, willing to supply the energy and grace to do what's right. Occasionally a child answers the question "no," giving me the opportunity to say, "While I'm working with you, one of my goals is to persuade you to become a Christian because of so many resources then available to you to help you do what's right."

As you help your children connect with God for themselves, you'll want to talk about the Holy Spirit, his role, and his desire to lead and empower your child. Following are some specific things to keep in mind.

1. *The Holy Spirit comes to live inside a person who has trusted Jesus as Savior and Lord.* And where does he live? He lives in the heart, the same place where the conscience is, along with a person's desires and emotions. In fact, the presence of the Holy Spirit inside you has a calming effect, producing a greater sense of peace and confidence on the inside. Furthermore, since the Holy Spirit lives on the inside, he is readily accessible, knows our inner thoughts, and helps us know God in personal ways. First Corinthians 2:10–12 says, "The Spirit searches all things, even the deep things of God. For who knows a person's thoughts except their own spirit within them? In the same way no one knows the thoughts of God except the Spirit of God. What we have received is not the spirit of the world, but the Spirit who is from God, so that we may understand what God has freely given us."

2. *The Holy Spirit empowers us to do what's right.* A child struggling with anger can call on God for peace and self-control, two of the nine qualities of the fruit of the Holy Spirit (Galatians 5:22–23). When a child must live with unfairness or the pressure of an irritating sibling, God provides strength to handle the situation well. Romans 8:26 tells us that "the Spirit helps us in our weakness."

> The Holy Spirit empowers us to do what's right.

God wants to provide us with strength to overcome our own desires to do the wrong thing. In fact, the greatest power you have to address impulses is the strength that comes from the Holy Spirit living within.

3. *The Holy Spirit prompts a child in the heart.* Sometimes that prompting is the conviction of sin, but other times it's a prompting for direction or guidance. When discussing

internal motivation with a child, it's helpful to ask, "What prompted you to go over and comfort that person? Was it your conscience making you feel uncomfortable because someone needed help? Or was it the Holy Spirit talking to you and giving you some direction?" Many children—and adults, for that matter—would have a hard time answering those questions, but it raises awareness of the reality that God is speaking if we will just listen. He talks to us in our hearts and prompts us to action. Sensitivity to the Holy Spirit's leadership produces greater internal motivation in a child's life.

4. *The Holy Spirit is our helper and teacher.* Just before Jesus left this earth, he told his disciples that he would be sending the Holy Spirit. John 14:26 says, "But the Helper, the Holy Spirit, whom the Father will send in my name, he will teach you all things and bring to your remembrance all that I have said to you" (esv). John 16:13 says, "But when he, the Spirit of truth, comes, he will guide you into all the truth." Children often don't know how to respond in a given situation. They need help. The Holy Spirit gives guidance on the spot. He prompts kids to do what's right.

Children, just like adults, need practice in order to properly interpret the internal messages in the heart. That's part of what it means to grow in the Christian life, but the sooner children learn to become aware of those promptings, the faster that growth can take place. God wants to speak to, teach, lead, and comfort your child. By talking about spiritual things and by discussing the interactive role of God in your own life, kids begin to experience that reality in their hearts as well.

The connection with God in our hearts is what we call *level three thinking.* It's always asking, "What is God doing here? What does he want *me* to do?" As the conscience pings a child's heart, sensitivity, awareness, and responsiveness create a heart that follows after God. When you go around the room and ask each person in your family, "What's one thing that God wants you to work on in your life?" you're drawing attention to the Holy Spirit's work.

> The connection with God in our hearts is what we call *level three thinking.*

That can be a special time as each person confesses an area of weakness and a prompting of God to make some changes. As you pray for one another, a spiritual connection takes place that raises the awareness of God's work in your child's life. The spiritual activity also draws your family closer together.

Jenni tells a touching story of how her family listened to God one evening:

> Last night we had an amazing time at the dinner table. My husband wasn't home yet, and so we had to eat without him. Judy, age four, said the table was lopsided because Daddy was missing.
>
> "Yes, it's sad to eat without Daddy."
>
> "But, Mom, God is always with us, so that means he is sitting in Daddy's chair, and we are not alone!"
>
> Then Elizabeth, our seven-year-old, had the idea of a new quiet game. "Let's be really quiet and listen to what God says to our minds and hearts." So we were silent. Amazingly, they both were still and concentrated on what they would hear from God. We then took turns sharing what we heard.
>
> Judy said she heard him say, "I love you, my child." Elizabeth was reminded of a special book we have read together for many years called *Mama, Do You Love Me?* The

best line in the book is the one that God brought to her mind, "I will love you forever and for always, because you are my dear one." I shared with them that God reminded me how special my children are and that they are gifts from him to be treasured. God reminded me how honored I am to be their mom and that I need to be the best mommy I can be.

Elizabeth then had the best idea of all. She said, "Mom, stand up and go over to the empty chair with us." So we all stood next to that chair. What happened next was one of the most precious mommy moments I have ever had. Elizabeth said, "Let's give God a big hug!" We all leaned over and hugged God, and although you might say we hugged a chair, no chair has ever felt so warm, so loving, or so emotion-provoking before in my life. It was truly a magical moment in the midst of an average evening dinner.

After we sat back down to eat, I was at a loss for words. What my girls had just helped me experience was truly a gift. They went on eating, and I choked down my food as I tried to hold my emotions together.

Elizabeth ended up switching seats because she wanted to sit on God's lap for dinner. The innocence of children amazes me, but more than that, their faith astounds me. There was no doubt, no question, no analyzing the situation. God came to dinner that night, and they welcomed him with open arms and taught their mom a thing or two in the process. Before I was a mom, I knew that I would have a lot to teach my children, but I'm learning more every day how much they have to teach me.

Does God speak to children? The answer is a definite "Yes!" God uses children to accomplish his work in the world. God used the little servant girl whose name isn't revealed in the Bible to point Naaman to God for healing. David killed Goliath while just a young man. Jesus used a boy's lunch to feed a whole multitude. God is looking for children who are willing to be used by him.

Samuel was a young boy when he went to live in the home of Eli the priest. In the middle of the night, God called his name, and after some guidance from Eli about listening, Samuel said to God, "Speak, LORD, for your servant is listening" (1 Samuel 3:9). That's exactly what we want to do with our kids: open up the pathways and free our kids up to hear from God and to build a personal, daily relationship with him.

19

Connecting Children to the Bible

The solution doesn't begin at the White House; the solution begins at my house.

I (Scott) had been working with Jake for several weeks on his meanness with his younger brother. Jake was fifteen, and the changes that needed to take place in his heart seemed to be stalled. On one particular visit, however, we began to see some progress. Here's how God worked in his life.

"Jake, how were things this week: better, worse, or the same?"

"The same."

His answer led me to believe that we needed a different approach.

"Jake, are you a Christian?"

"Yes."

"Does God speak to you?"

"No."

"Would you like him to?"

"I think so."

"Okay. Open the Bible on my iPad there to Philippians 2:3–4, and let's see what God has to say. Go ahead and read it."

Jake opened the Bible and read, "'Do nothing out of selfish ambition or vain conceit. Rather, in humility value others above yourselves, not looking to your own interests but each of you to the interests of the others.'"

"What is God saying to you there?"

"I don't know."

"Here. Give me the Bible. I'm going to demonstrate to you how God speaks. He's going to speak to me right now. Watch." I read the verses, and then I paused and shared my reflection. "God is reminding me of two things. First, my wife has an impor-

> The Scriptures are unlike any other book you might come across.

tant event this week, and I need to think about her interests, not just about my own. Second, you're sitting across from me, and I need to value you above myself. That means that even though I'm a counselor, I need to treat you like a king's kid. God has spoken to me today. Here. You try." I handed the iPad back to him.

Jake looked at the verses, and you could see the wheels turning in his head. "I think God wants me to share my video game with my brother."

"Great. God is speaking to you, Jake. There's a second question, though, that you need to ask. It's this: If God speaks, are you willing to listen?"

Jake was on the right track. The key would be connecting Jake's heart to God's Word so he could grow in his ability to respond better to his brother.

The Scriptures are unlike any other book you might come across. Kids may learn and become inspired by reading other books or hearing a story from the newspaper, but the Bible has an unusual power to change the human heart. Ephesians 5:26 says that the Scriptures help clean us up, "washing with water through the word." The Bible keeps us from sin. Psalm 119:9 says, "How can a young man keep his way pure? By living according to your word." The reality is that the Bible is a living tool that touches us in the most important part of our being: the heart.

Hidden in the Heart

In order for the Bible to do its work in the hearts of children, it's important to expose them to it in ways they can understand. Psalm 119:11 says, "I have hidden your word in my heart that I might not sin against you." Hiding the Bible in a child's heart can be done in a number of ways. Family Time often helps move the content of a Bible story from the head down to the heart because of its emphasis on practical application.

God gave us his Word to transfer the mind of God to the hearts of people, resulting in a lifestyle of practical service for him. The Bible contains truths that must be understood in the context of their intent. Not everyone understands this. Some come to the Bible as a book of quotations or believe that whatever impression they get after reading a passage is from God. That's a dangerous approach to the Scriptures. It puts the authority in the mind of the reader instead of in the Scriptures themselves.

The Bible must be understood in its context. The process of studying God's Word to determine what it means in its context is called *interpretation*. Once the meaning is established, then the student of God's Word looks for principles out of which applications flow.

It's not a wise approach to say, "This is what this passage means to me" when talking about the interpretation of Scripture. The Bible has one intended interpretation, but several principles, and many applications. The one interpretation may be in question at times as different people try to determine what that one true meaning is, but when we come to the Bible, we seek to first understand what God means by the words on the page. Then we can apply the message personally.

One Interpretation, Many Applications

The application of God's truth will vary from one individual to another. One dad illustrated this by talking with his son about Ephesians 4:15: "Instead, speaking the truth in love, we will in all things grow up into him who is the Head, that is, Christ." What does God mean in that passage? The context reveals that God is contrasting a childish approach with a more mature approach. Speaking the truth in love is a result of mature thinking. After discussing the context, they next talked about how to apply it together. Dad determined that he needed to be loving in his approach, even when he was right. Gordy, his twelve-year-old son, realized that he tended to try to please people and be more loving when sometimes he needed to emphasize the truth. The applications of God's Word differed, but the truth remained the same.

> One of the reasons the Scriptures are alive is because the applications vary and fit new or different situations.

One of the reasons the Scriptures are alive is because the applications vary and fit new or different situations. One person may read the Bible today and see ways to put it into practice that are different from the ways they practiced it last week or last month. The Scriptures are powerful, and when kids understand that, reading God's Word becomes an adventure.

Memorizing Bible verses is a powerful way to get God's

Word into a person's life. Sometimes parents pull away from memorization because their children may not understand the words they're saying. And they're right. Kids may not understand, but having those words in memory often allows God to use them over the years as a garden of biblical truth growing in the heart. If the Bible verses are just parroted back to receive an award, then kids may view the Scriptures as superficial, not recognizing their vast depth and importance. But that shouldn't stop parents from helping their children memorize Scriptures. Rather, it should be motivation to take those words and look for ways to apply them to life.

Memorization Is Strategic

One pastor told this story: "I grew up in a Christian home where, thanks to my parents and good children's programs, I memorized about two hundred Scripture verses as a preschooler and about fifteen hundred Bible verses by the time I graduated from high school. I certainly didn't understand all that I memorized, especially as a young child. If you asked me today how many of those verses I remember, I'm not sure. But I do know this. There are times when I'm counseling with someone and I remember, 'There's a verse about that.' The words are somewhere in my memory and remind me to go to the Scripture and find the verse. When I'm tempted or need encouragement, I often remember a Bible verse. Maybe not the exact words, sometimes, but the idea of that verse comes back to me and gives me just what I need at that moment."

Memorizing God's Word is an investment in one's future. Little nuggets of truth are embedded in the mind. Then God, over time, transfers those truths to the heart. It's actually amazing to come across a Bible story or verse again and discover new meaning as the application hits home.

God provided his Word for every human heart. That means that the Bible was written for you, and it was written for your kids. In fact, as you go through passages in the Bible, it often seems as if God included that verse just for you, and he did. The Bible is a personal book, not simply a book of history or instructions. It's a personal book with practical applications to the daily situations your children face.

Memorizing God's Word is an investment in one's future.

One mom was helping her son deal with his anger and said, "I think God placed a passage in the Bible just for you." When he gave her a puzzled look, she said, "Check out Ephesians 4:31–32." He looked it up, and it said, "Get rid of all bitterness, rage and anger, brawling and slander, along with every form of malice. Be kind and compassionate to one another, forgiving each other, just as in Christ God forgave you." They discussed together the six different types of anger named in that passage, and Mom used that opportunity to help her son understand that when he chose to avoid anger and chose kindness instead, he was being like God. What an awesome thought for an eight-year-old.

One of the main goals of childhood is for kids to begin to understand God's ways and learn to walk in them. Kids can learn to think biblically, but to do that, they need regular exposure to the Bible and its teaching. The Scriptures have a way of conforming our thinking to the heart of God. Kids learn that the Bible speaks to many facets of life and is relevant for daily decision making.

Kids Can Initiate Spiritually

It's interesting that in the Old Testament, part of the responsibility for initiating spiritually rested with the children. Joshua 4 follows the exciting story of the Israelites crossing over the Jordan River on dry ground to enter the promised land. After God gave instructions to Joshua to build a monument of stones from the riverbed, he made an interesting statement: "In the future, when your children ask you, 'What do these stones mean?' tell them . . ." (vv. 6–7). The children are asking the questions.

But today kids often don't know what questions to ask. You may want to give them a list. For example, does your child know of the events that led up to your commitment to Christ? That's a good place to start. You have monument stones in your life that stand as a testimony to God's power and grace. Kids need to hear those stories. Not only are they interesting, but they're often an application of God's truth.

Kids need a balanced perspective of God's Word. Some parents overemphasize the corrective aspect of the Scriptures, pulling out verses that help kids see what they did wrong and how they missed the mark of God's standard. Although this may be helpful on occasion, if that's the dominant message children receive, then they get a skewed view of the Bible and can develop a misunderstanding of God's character.

Furthermore, the Bible isn't just a book about moral teaching. We're not just trying to get our kids to act the right way using God's Word as a standard. The Bible is a book about God connecting with the human heart, desiring internal change, not just outward performance.

The Bible plays several different roles in our lives. Second Timothy 3:16 says, "All Scripture is God-breathed and is useful for teaching, rebuking, correcting and training in righteousness." Not only does the Bible rebuke us, but it teaches and trains us as well. It also affirms that we are children of God. Sometimes parents can pass on a message of affirmation to a child that comes from God himself. One mom said to her twelve-year-old daughter, "Did you know that God loves you just the way you are?" That was an interesting thought for her daughter, who tended to put herself down and measure herself by her weaknesses. The fact that God loved her right now,

> Sometimes parents can pass on a message of affirmation to a child that comes from God himself.

in the process of growing, was just what she needed in order to deal with some of the discouragement she was feeling.

The Bible provides solutions for life, and kids can find direction for their days. One fourteen-year-old boy decided that God wanted him to ask more questions about how others were feeling instead of focusing on how he was feeling. He was motivated by Philippians 2:4: "Each of you should look not only to your own interests, but also to the interests of others." He realized he could be a better friend by thinking about others instead of focusing so much on himself.

Four Areas of Theology to Cover with Kids

Most of the interaction about faith with children falls into four areas of conversation. The beauty of these four areas is that although they can be very deep theological truths, they're also very simple, allowing even those who have just come to Christ to talk about them and share them with *their* kids. Here are the four areas to include as you pass the faith on to your child.

1. *God.* Give them an understanding of the Father, Jesus, and the Holy Spirit and their respective personal works in our lives.

2. *Man.* Help them recognize our unique creation, sinful nature, and divine purpose.
3. *The Bible.* It is God's standard of moral authority, and it determines right and wrong, provides understanding of our purpose, and gives guidance for daily living.
4. *The Plan.* Share with them the importance of embracing salvation, discipleship, and a mission-oriented view of life individually, as a family, and in the Christian community.

Some may argue that theology is more complex than that, and certainly it can be. However, it's not necessary for you to have all the answers to every theological question before you begin sharing spiritually with your children. You'll likely run into questions that force you to find answers yourself. But that's part of what it means to be growing in Christ. And your search for answers is a wonderful example to your children of your continually growing faith.

Your Home Is a Discipleship Center

Growing in God's grace is not just for kids. We're all children of God. Even though God has set up parents to be the authority in the home, there's a very real sense in which parents and children are walking alongside one another in their spiritual journeys. Parents are intentionally passing the faith on to children, and kids can encourage their parents in godliness as well.

It's fun to watch God speak to kids. One of the ways to encourage them to listen to God is to ask them what God is teaching them. Kids who are new to the idea of listening to God speak may need a bit of encouragement. When you ask your child, "Does God speak to you?" what is the answer? We've already seen that God speaks through his Word, but God also speaks through the conscience, or through a parent, or provides an impression during prayer.

You might say to your daughter on the way to church, "I'll be eager to hear what God says to you today in children's church." Then, after church, ask her. Church gatherings are designed to be a place where people meet with God, not just their friends. When you share a lesson learned or listen to a child talk about a church experience, God may speak through your discussion.

Rick talked to his son on the way home from church. "Miguel, what did you learn at church today?"

"We learned about Noah."

Dad gave his son a puzzled look.

"What?" his son said. "You know, the story about Noah and the ark."

"I didn't mean, 'What did the teacher teach?' I meant, 'What did God say to you today?'"

His son didn't know what to say. Dad felt he had made his point, and he left it at that, but a few minutes later his son picked up the conversation again.

"I learned that God asks people to do hard things."

Dad had forgotten the discussion momentarily, but then remembered what his son was talking about. "What kind of hard things does God ask you to do?"

That question opened up a whole discussion about how Miguel could obey God in practical ways as he related to his annoying brother and worked on completing his next badge for Boy Scouts.

Rick helped his son connect with God's Word in ways that were surprising to both of them.

It's these kinds of conversations that God had in mind when he told the Deuteronomy believers to impress the commands on the hearts of their children as they walked along the road, got up in the morning, sat in their homes, and went to bed at night. These informal conversations about life and God and his Word help children understand what it means to be a disciple of Jesus Christ and to develop level three thinking.

> Rick helped his son connect with God's Word in ways that were surprising to both of them.

In short, passing the faith on to your kids increases family closeness, puts everyone on the same team, and helps develop kids who are following God and are committed to serving others. The family is a place of growth where both parents and children explore, learn, fail, experience forgiveness, and practice following God in daily life.

The home is a disciple-making center. It's in the family that children learn what it means to be a Christian, to follow Jesus, and to live a life guided by him.

But what if you are a single parent or if your mate isn't on the same page? That's a great question and one that needs to be addressed in order to inspire the parent who feels a lack of support. In fact, most of the time one parent will feel a greater passion for spiritual training in the home. We've written the next chapter to encourage you as you try to make changes in your family.

20

Going It Solo

Every parent has influence and relationship.
Don't minimize those two facts, but be sure to
use them to pass on the faith to your kids.

Diane was discouraged. She had attended one of our parenting seminars and realized that a heart-based approach to parenting was so important. In fact, she had been trying to do some of the things taught in the seminar, and she wanted to do so much more. But her husband wasn't a believer. He wasn't working together with her to teach godly values to their kids. Diane was struggling inside. "I just feel like I can't get anywhere if my husband isn't working with me."

When spouses are on the same page, passing the faith on to kids can be a team effort, but sometimes that isn't the case. Many times Mom and Dad aren't even in the same book. It may be that the other parent isn't a Christian, or isn't interested, or simply isn't there or available. Because this problem is so common and because it tends to discourage parents, we've dedicated a complete chapter to address it.

The Power of Dad

When it comes to raising children, the Bible has some specific things to say to dads. Ephesians 6:4 says, "Fathers, do not exasperate your children; instead, bring them up in the training and instruction of the Lord." Furthermore, when it comes to the marriage relationship, husbands have a spiritual responsibility to their wives. Ephesians 5:25–28 says, "Husbands, love your wives, just as Christ loved the church and gave himself up for her to make her holy, cleansing her by the washing with water through the word, and to present her to himself as a radiant church, without stain or wrinkle or any other blemish, but holy and blameless. In this same way, husbands ought to love their wives as their own bodies."

> When dads take spiritual initiative in the home, everyone feels a greater sense of direction and security.

The Bible is clear that the husband has a significant spiritual influence on family life. If you're a husband or father reading this, you'll want to take your biblical responsibility seriously. Your commitment to Jesus Christ will demonstrate itself in the way you work with your family.

When dads take spiritual initiative in the home, everyone feels a greater sense of direction and security. In fact, many dimensions of God's character are learned through the modeling of good fatherhood. It's interesting that God chose the picture of the father to describe the kind of relationship he wants to have with us. Dads are a balance of many character qualities all at the same time. They teach love by their attention to needs. They teach holiness by emphasizing right and wrong, and they teach about forgiveness by ending discipline times positively. They also demonstrate the encouragement and leadership of the Holy

Spirit as they teach children the importance of Scripture and of relying on it. Dads have a powerful influence in the home. Your spiritual initiative is very important for family life, and you have many good things to offer that contribute to your family's spiritual strength.

The Power of Mom

A mom has the ability to touch a child's heart in a very special way. That's likely why God gives instructions in Titus 2:4 for older women to teach younger women, among other things, to love their husbands and children. Proverbs 31 is an acrostic using the letters of the Hebrew alphabet to detail the perfect wife and mother. Although no one woman can embody all these traits, they're a model for women to follow. Most of the description has to do with her personal and household energy. The point is that there's much a mother can do to help the family do well. And notice verse 1, which tells where this teaching came from: a mother taught this material to her son, who passed it on to us.

In 1 Samuel 1–2, Hannah took spiritual initiative in her family, resulting in God's blessing of a child for them. Proverbs 1:8 says, "Listen, my son, to your father's instruction and do not forsake your mother's teaching." These passages make it clear that the role of a mom is significant in a family. If you're a mom reading these words, remember that your spiritual initiative is necessary and helpful for your family's strength. God has given you some specific gifts, insight, and knowledge that your family needs.

Flying Solo

When a husband and wife are in agreement in their desire to pass the faith on to their children and can act in a coordinated way, the whole family benefits. But what about families, like Diane's, where only one of the parents is interested in spiritual things? Maybe only one of the parents is a Christian, or you're a single parent, or the other parent is a Christian but doesn't take spiritual initiative. Or maybe a parent is removed from the family for a time. Instead of focusing on what you don't have, it's best to focus on the spiritual influence you do have. If you're married, then regular prayer for your mate is strategic in God's plan for family life. As you look for ways to initiate spiritually with your mate and your children, rely on God's grace and ask him to provide the right things to say and do.

It's sometimes tempting for a parent to give up on spiritual initiative in the home because of a lack of partnership or a lack of spiritual sensitivity of a mate. The best thing you can do is recognize the power you have as a dad or mom to influence your family spiritually. In fact, you have a calling to continue to influence your children even if you don't have a partner willing to participate.

There's an interesting story in the Old Testament about a father who was not providing spiritual leadership in his home, so the mother took charge, and God blessed the situation. The man was Moses. In Exodus 4:24–26, we have a short little story about Moses getting ready to lead God's people out of Egypt. He was about to do a great work, but he hadn't been a spiritual leader in his own home. He hadn't circumcised his son. God was angry, and the Bible says that "the LORD met [Moses] and was about to kill him." Obviously, God takes spiritual leadership in the home seriously, especially if one is called to lead God's people.

In that moment, Zipporah, Moses' wife, stepped up to remedy the situation. She circumcised their son, and God was satisfied. The interesting dynamic in the story is that a wife's spiritual initiative with the child saved her husband. I'm sure that many a husband today is grateful for his wife's spiritual initiative in the home.

In the New Testament, we read of Timothy's "sincere faith," passed down to him by his grandmother and his mother (2 Timothy 1:5). Where was Dad? We know from Acts 16:3 that his dad was a Greek. We don't know if he was a Christian, but we do know that his mother and grandmother were more notable in his spiritual development.

> God takes spiritual leadership in the home seriously, especially if one is called to lead God's people.

As Diane heard us share these things, you could see her countenance change. Hope was reentering her heart. But she needed some practical ideas about how to add spirituality in her home. So we gave her some ideas that helped her develop a specific plan for her home. That plan will change over time, but Diane gained hope that God can use her in her family.

Use Your Influence Wisely

On a practical level, if your spouse doesn't support your faith, look for non-offensive ways to influence your children. Many dads or moms who don't tend to lead spiritually are willing to sit in on a Family Time and even find it exciting and engaging. Although they don't want to lead the spiritual exercises, they may be willing to participate. In some homes, however, a mate may be hostile to spiritual training and refuse to allow the other parent to dialogue openly about it. In those situations you'll want to look for ways to pass on the faith to your child that doesn't overtly offend your mate. One mom said she drives the kids to school in the morning, and she uses that time to share a Bible verse for the day with her kids.

Your level of spiritual initiative is directly related to the amount of influence you have in the situation. If you only see your kids every other weekend and a couple of days in between, then that's your arena of influence. Plan it wisely and use it well. The reality is that you have influence with your kids. As you incorporate who you are as a Christ-follower in that arena, kids pick it up. Eventually those children will have to choose a value system for themselves. They'll have seen you model discipleship in your life over the years and will have a basis upon which to choose for themselves.

> Your level of spiritual initiative is directly related to the amount of influence you have in the situation.

Don't allow your limitations to influence your vision. In fact, God works through our weaknesses. He often uses limitations and challenges to fulfill his vision. Faith under pressure shines brighter in a dark world. Sometimes what looks like a major setback is part of something bigger that God is doing. Queen Esther had a number of limitations in her life. Yet, when all looked hopeless and impossible—so much so that it didn't seem worthwhile to even try—her uncle Mordecai said to her, "Who knows but that you have come to royal position for such a time as this?" (Esther 4:14). And indeed, God used her mightily to save the Israelite people.

We often don't realize the significance of one person's dedication in achieving God's purposes. The reality is that God loves your children. He has a plan for their lives. He gives you an opportunity to influence their lives for just a short time. As you seek the Lord and take initiative to discern where God is working in their lives, you can pass the faith on to your kids. Sometimes it's only small seeds that are nurtured later in other contexts. Other times it's a whole garden that you can share, and it brings forth flowers of blessing over the years.

God is good. Every day when you get up, trust him and commit yourself to him. It's very possible that today may provide another opportunity for you to shine for Jesus in a rather challenging situation.

21

Will You Take the Family Challenge?

Send your son to church—spiritually
feed him for a day. Live it out at home—
spiritually feed him for life.

B rian was ready. You could tell by the tone of his voice that
he was eager to move forward but was a bit apprehensive as
well. "Okay. I'm sold. Tell me what I need to do. I realize I need
to exercise more spiritual leadership in my home. What do I do
next? I have a feeling that it'll be best for me to start with me
first. Any ideas?"

"Yes, working on yourself is the best." And much of what
we share in this chapter inspired Brian to move forward to provide more spiritual interaction in his home. We've discussed the
importance of passing on the faith, given you tools, and provided helpful strategies to make it happen. But simply reading
about it doesn't impact the family. It's the action that has a lasting influence. Here's how you can prepare your heart to take the
Family Challenge.

Be Intentional

Taking the Family Challenge simply means being intentional about passing the faith on to your kids, both spontaneously as opportunities arise and through at least one structured Family Time each week. The Family Challenge contains three ingredients: *building relationship*, *sharing Scripture*, and *practicing faith*. As you determine to do these three things, your kids will see more clearly what it means to follow God and serve him wholeheartedly. Take a minute and pray that God will give you direction and wisdom as you take on the Family Challenge. Decide now before you read further. What will be your next step?

> There's nothing like a plan for energizing you to action.

Most parents have parenting books sitting on their shelves that they haven't read. Still more have books that they've read but haven't put into action. It may be good to develop a specific, measurable plan for using something that you've learned in these pages. There's nothing like a plan for energizing you to action. A plan provides a goal, the next steps, and hope to move forward in the face of challenges.

Change in a family will always meet resistance. People find themselves in patterns, and even if those patterns aren't the best, people tend to stay in them because they're familiar. If you're going to make some changes, you'll need to persevere for several weeks. Over time, you'll help your family act differently, think differently, and learn to trust God for the challenges they'll face.

Like Brian, we must all realize that any call to commitment is a challenge to one's own heart. The heart contains things like desires, commitment, emotions, passion, and convictions. Just because something comes from the heart, though, doesn't make it good. Some people's desires or emotions prompt them to put off goals, give up when facing challenges, or take on other commitments that compete with the most important things in their lives.

To help you establish your desire to move forward to intentionally pass on the faith to your kids, let's look at three words that describe essential things that are developed in the heart: *conviction*, *commitment*, and *passion*. When your heart is in it, there's very little that can deter you from making progress toward your goal. You'll need all three of these as you take the Family Challenge in your home.

Conviction

The Bible teaches that convictions are established in the heart. A *conviction* is a belief that's so important that it results in action. You know the story of Daniel. He was certainly a man of conviction. The Bible tells us, "Daniel purposed *in his heart* that he would not defile himself" (Daniel 1:8 KJV). When Jeremiah described the new covenant that God would establish, he wrote that it would be different from the stone tablets of the old covenant. God said, "I will put my law in their minds and write it on their hearts" (Jeremiah 31:33). Notice, in both of these passages, that convictions develop in the heart and then result in outward actions. We know that beliefs are embraced in the heart because Paul describes salvation in terms of a heart commitment. Romans 10:9 says a key to salvation is that you "believe in your heart that God raised [Jesus] from the dead."

Convictions are essential because they help manage emotions and desires, two other facets of the heart. If your *desire* to do something contrary to your goal is *high*, and your *conviction* is *low*, then you will be tempted to do that other thing, rather than work toward your goal. When your *convictions* are stronger than your emotions and desires, you can persist when you don't feel like it or when you'd rather do something else. An inner conviction prompts you to strive toward your goal and not be distracted or led astray.

When you believe that your child's heart is the key, that God has placed a conscience in your child's heart that needs training, that God's Word is the standard and is practical for kids, and that the Holy Spirit seeks to guide your child personally to develop a healthy sense of internal motivation, you've got the basic understanding necessary to propel you forward with a sense of conviction. Training children spiritually is not optional. There's an urgency about reaching your child's heart with the message of God's plan. If you develop strong convictions to take action in this area, you'll be far more successful at building a new culture in your family.

Brian knew he needed to move forward. He was developing some personal convictions, but he felt that they weren't strong enough. He decided that he needed to spend time with God each day to be ready to talk to his kids. That belief prompted him to listen on his iPhone to three chapters of the Bible each day on his way to work. Sometimes he'd listen to more and sometimes less, but when he arrived at work, he would take two minutes in the parking lot and write down a lesson learned that would be helpful for his family. His journal became a treasure. It often just contained the Scripture reference and a few lines of application, but he found himself going back to his writing over and over again in family conversations. His conviction that it is important to spend time with God made passing on the faith much easier.

Commitment

Commitment, like conviction, starts in the heart. Proverbs 3:5 says, "Trust in the LORD with all your heart." That internal desire to put God first happens deep inside a person, but it often meets other internal struggles. Commitment keeps a person on course. It is a choice. In order to take the Family Challenge, you'll need to be committed to the process and stick with it when resistance and distractions threaten your plans. It's amazing how one person can change a family when an underlying commitment comes from the heart.

> It's amazing how one person can change a family when an underlying commitment comes from the heart.

Many obstacles will likely get in the way of your progress. Things like busyness, bad attitudes, and resistance from a spouse are likely to slow you down at times, but your ability to hang in there after you feel like quitting is directly related to your heart. Moses knew that God's people would face many challenges when they entered the promised land, so he challenged them to make a commitment in their hearts to God's commands. He said, "Take to heart all the words I have solemnly declared to you this day . . . They are your life" (Deuteronomy 32:46–47).

Your heart is the place where it all starts. As you allow the Lord to speak to you, he will bring your heart to a place of strong commitment, so strong that you'll be able to do the work, overcome the challenges, and face the obstacles necessary for change. It won't be long before God begins to work in the hearts of other family members, and your prayer is that, one by one, they, too, will develop a commitment to the time you spend as a family talking about God's Word.

As part of his commitment, Brian asked his wife to help. She was willing, as long as he continued to take the lead. They determined that they would pray together once a week. During that twenty- to thirty-minute meeting, they would look at the schedule and pray for their kids. They announced to the children that they were praying for them, and even asked for specific requests that they could bring before the Lord. At first, the kids shared trivial things, but over time, prayer became integral in all of their lives. The commitment of these parents moved prayer to a central place in their home and resulted in a number of conversations about God's grace, power, and provision.

Passion

A third word to help you move forward is *passion*. It's interesting to see the number of times passion is revealed in the Bible as coming from the heart. Hezekiah was a good king who served the Lord with all his heart (2 Chronicles 31:21 ESV). David said in Psalms, "I will praise you, O LORD, with all my heart" (9:1) and "I seek you with all my heart" (119:10). In each of these verses, the word *heart* communicates the idea of passion.

> When people do something wholeheartedly, they're doing it with zest and determination.

When people do something wholeheartedly, they're doing it with zest and determination. Sometimes we say, "He put his heart into the job" or "She has a heart for what she's doing." Passion combines commitment, convictions, and emotion to drive the plan toward the goal.

Children see their parents' passion when it comes to sports, money, or a hobby. Do they see that same passion about Jesus Christ? Brian, reporting about his childhood, told this story to his kids: "My mom loved Jesus. Every Saturday morning she would gather us kids around her, and she would tell us stories from the Bible. She kept us captivated as she talked about victories, tragic mistakes, and miracles in people's lives. While she talked, she'd peel apples. Each week she would peel and cut those apples and turn them into the best apple cobbler I ever tasted. Still today I have sweet memories of God's grace and power every time I smell apples and cinnamon cooking. My mother's passion for God's Word was contagious, and now I enjoy reading it to you. I don't peel apples, but I want you kids to know that I love Jesus just like your grandmother did."

Now Is the Time

Do you believe that God has given you the opportunity and the responsibility to pass the faith on to your kids? If you do, make it more than a belief. Turn it into a *conviction*. Make it a *commitment*. Allow *passion* to fuel your goals and plans to move forward. Then watch God do some amazing things in your family.

It'll be fun to see what happens to *you* first, and then the little surprises that come from your kids. One little boy came to his mom and said, "Mom, I was starting to get mad, and I put myself in a break to settle down. Now I'm fine." Those words were a treasure since Mom had been trying to help her son deal with anger. They had talked about James 1:19, which says, "Everyone should be quick to listen, slow to speak and slow to become angry." Mom was seeing God work in her five-year-old son. He had a long way to go, but she was encouraged that God was doing a deeper work in his life already.

Many of the rewards of passing on the faith to your kids come over a period of time. You're creating a godly heritage and a faith legacy that kids will use as a foundation for years to come. The early spiritual training children receive as teens or elementary-age children, or even preschoolers, creates a vital lifeline for their own personal faith. Kids learn that God has solutions for every area of their lives. As they grow up, they'll continue to put their faith into practice. They'll see that God's Word has implications for the office, for a marriage, for friendships, and for conflict, money, and health. They'll learn to integrate their faith into life in some relevant and practical ways.

> You're creating a godly heritage and a faith legacy that kids will use as a foundation for years to come.

For now, though, you're building a spiritual foundation for your children. Are you committed? If so, we want to ask you to join with others around the world who are expressing their commitment to pass the faith on to their kids by taking the Family Challenge. These parents and grandparents are committing themselves to God and to their kids. They're committing to intentionally *build relationship*, *share Scripture*, and *practice faith*. Take a moment and go to www.414familychallenge.com and add your commitment to hundreds of others. Then look at the map and see how God is working in the lives of parents and grandparents all over the world to pass the faith on to their kids.

At the National Center for Biblical Parenting, we have a vision to empower parents to pass the faith on to their kids and to mobilize churches to equip them. We're on a mission both in the United States and around the world. We believe the most strategic way to make that happen is through parents. Start in your own family to pass the faith on to your kids, and then determine to spread the word about the value of the family as a discipleship center.

Conclusion

Nurturing Hope

A teaspoon of hope provides enough fuel
to dig through the biggest mountain.

P arenting is an awesome responsibility. You love your kids
and desperately want them to grow in their walk with the
Lord. You want them to love God and serve him with all their
hearts. You likely see weaknesses that frustrate you, and even
scare you at times, but you look for ways to challenge your kids
to move forward. One of the things
that can help you do that is to keep
your focus on the goal.

Moral and spiritual
development in
children prepare
them for life.

This book has been about the
goal of passing the faith on to your
children and giving them a strong conscience to help them *stay
true to their convictions.* Moral and spiritual development in
children prepare them for life. Your kids will face many challenges, just as you have. The question is, will they have the

internal strength to match the challenge? As you implement the tools suggested in this book and develop your parenting using a heart-based approach, you will help your children become disciples of Christ.

God Provides the Hope

Sometimes the daily challenges of life bring discouragement to the heart of a weary parent. Remember that God has given you spiritual resources to help in those moments. The freedom to pray, share with a friend, and experience the peace that comes from the Holy Spirit can all keep you going during stressful times. And God's own grace will fill your heart when emotional reserves are low. In those moments it's especially critical to remember the importance of relying on God instead of on your own strength.

God is our hope, and he sometimes uses challenging situations to build our hearts. But Romans 5:3–5 reminds us that we are to "rejoice in our sufferings because we know that suffering produces perseverance; perseverance, character; and character, hope. And hope does not disappoint us, because God has poured out his love into our hearts by the Holy Spirit, whom he has given us." The challenges of parenting often build character in us and increase our hope in the process.

Always put your hope in the Lord. Parenting is a humbling experience. Kids at times can embarrass, disappoint, frustrate, and discourage their parents. In those times it's important to rely on God's grace that he pours out to us in abundance. Always remember that your job isn't to produce results. It's to be faithful and allow God to produce the fruit. You want to have a clear conscience before God in your own life regarding your parenting. Where you've failed, ask forgiveness from God and from your children. Do what's right now, even though it's hard. Commit yourself to God, and look for ways to pass your faith on to your children. Those are the most important ways to influence your family at any age. First, obey God yourself, and then seek to make disciples of your children. And with God's help and grace, he will enable you to do it.

> You want to have a clear conscience before God in your own life regarding your parenting.

But hope isn't just for parents. Kids need hope too. They tend to see life as it is right now. They focus on what they want and become discouraged when they fail or don't get it. Along with all the firmness and boundaries, love and dialogue, make sure that part of your parenting energy is dedicated to developing hope in your child. Kids need to have a vision for what life can look like, the freedom to learn from mistakes, and the support and encouragement to continue on even when they've had a bad day.

It may even be helpful for you and your child to memorize verses about hope in God's Word. A favorite is Jeremiah 29:11, "'For I know the plans I have for you,' declares the LORD, 'plans to prosper you and not to harm you, plans to give you hope and a future.'" The next two verses reveal the key to experiencing that promise: "Call upon me and come and pray to me, and I will listen to you. You will seek me and find me when you seek me with all your heart."

As children understand what it actually means to serve and follow God, powerful things happen in their hearts. It's amazing to watch children grow spiritually. They learn to pray, listen to God, and seek to follow him. When kids are empowered spiritually, great things happen.

In this book we've tried to give you a vision for something big. By understanding how God made us and how he wants to work in every person's life, you'll be able to help your children in more strategic ways. Moral and spiritual development in children is paramount for their future. Many parents today miss this whole dimension of child training. But as you engage, day after day, in the hard work of disciple-making, you will begin to see the fruits of your labor. And in time, your faithful efforts will have an impact that lasts for eternity.

Index

255

Scripture Index

About the Authors

Scott Turansky graduated with two master's degrees from Western Conservative Baptist Seminary and a Doctor of Ministry from Fuller Theological Seminary. He has been a pastor and missionary for more than thirty-three years and is an author of several books. In addition to pastoring full-time, Scott also conducts parenting seminars on Fridays and Saturdays around the US (http://www.biblicalparenting.org/).

He is the cofounder of the National Center for Biblical Parenting and has coauthored twelve books. He has also coauthored three video parent training programs used in churches around the country and has written three children's programs for families and churches to use with kids. Scott is married to Carrie and has five children.

Joanne Miller is a registered nurse with more than twenty-five years of pediatric experience. She is also a cofounder of the

National Center for Biblical Parenting and coauthor of twelve parenting books. Joanne and her husband, Ed, have two grown sons. She enjoys teaching parenting seminars around the country and overseeing much of the day-to-day operations for the National Center for Biblical Parenting.

If you like **Motivate Your Child**, then you'll love the other resources in the series.

Hero Training Camp

is the Conscience Development Program for Kids. Use this curriculum in your home or a group to help kids understand the promptings of the conscience using games, Bible stories, activities, snacks, and crafts.

The video-based parent training program **Everyday Parents CAN Raise Extraordinary Kids** will take your small group through an understanding of internal motivation, the conscience and the Holy Spirit, and provide interactive discussion that's practical and biblical.

biblicalparenting.org/motivateyourchild

Free
E-mail Parenting
Tips

Receive guidance and inspiration a couple of times a week in your inbox. Free Parenting Tips give practical suggestions to help you relate better to your kids and help your kids change their hearts, not just their behavior.

The National Center for Biblical Parenting is here to help you. Visit biblicalparenting.org and sign up today for Free E-mail Parenting Tips, available in English and Spanish. While you're there, discover other great resources for parents.

76 Hopatcong Drive, Lawrenceville, NJ 08648-4136
Phone: (609) 771-8002
E-mail: parent@biblicalparenting.org
Web: biblicalparenting.org